FOREWORD BY SIDDHARTH RAJSEKAR

THE
SILENT
PATH

A Journey Within

CHERAG SHAH

CLEVER FOX PUBLISHING
Chennai, India

Published by CLEVER FOX PUBLISHING 2025
Copyright © Cherag Shah 2025

All Rights Reserved.
ISBN: 978-93-67075-34-0

This book has been published with all reasonable efforts taken to make the material error-free after the consent of the author. No part of this book shall be used, reproduced in any manner whatsoever without written permission from the author, except in the case of brief quotations embodied in critical articles and reviews.

The Author of this book is solely responsible and liable for its content including but not limited to the views, representations, descriptions, statements, information, opinions and references ["Content"]. The Content of this book shall not constitute or be construed or deemed to reflect the opinion or expression of the Publisher or Editor. Neither the Publisher nor Editor endorse or approve the Content of this book or guarantee the reliability, accuracy or completeness of the Content published herein and do not make any representations or warranties of any kind, express or implied, including but not limited to the implied warranties of merchantability, fitness for a particular purpose. The Publisher and Editor shall not be liable whatsoever for any errors, omissions, whether such errors or omissions result from negligence, accident, or any other cause or claims for loss or damages of any kind, including without limitation, indirect or consequential loss or damage arising out of use, inability to use, or about the reliability, accuracy or sufficiency of the information contained in this book.

CONTENTS

Foreword — xi
Introduction — xv

CHAPTER 1. WEIGHT OF THE WORLD — 1
    The Weight of Expectations — 2
    The First Step — 4
    Packing More Than a Bag — 7
    Conversations with Myself — 8
    The Departure — 9
    The Arrival in Rishikesh — 12

CHAPTER 2. RIVER'S CALL — 15
    The First Encounter — 16
    The Ganga Aarti — 19
    The encounter with the stranger — 21
    The Unexpected News — 24
    The Decision to Stay — 25
    An Invitation — 27

CHAPTER 3. THE TREK WITHIN — 29
    The First Steps — 30
    The First Breakthrough — 32
    Into the Unknown — 34
    The Steeper Path — 36
    A Moment of Pause — 38

Contents

CHAPTER 4. SILENCE AS A TEACHER — 40
   The Noise Within — 40
   A Lesson from Nature — 41
   The Language of Silence — 42
   The Stillness Ahead — 43
   The Weight of Stillness — 44
   Learning from the Mountains — 47
   A Step Toward Stillness — 49
   A Mirror to the Soul — 50
   A Shared Stillness — 53

CHAPTER 5. ARRIVAL AT THE CAVES — 56
   The Last Ascent — 56
   The First Glimpse — 58
   A Sacred Welcome — 60
   A Name Revealed — 61
   The Seven Monk's — 64
   Completing the Circle — 68
   The Power of Stillness — 69
   The Depth of Surrender — 70
   The River as a Metaphor — 72

CHAPTER 6. BREATH AS THE BRIDGE — 77
   The Breath: A Portal — 77
   Process of Conscious Breathing — 79
   Breath as a Mirror — 80
   The Prana-Shakti Connection — 81
   The Breath of Life — 82

Breath as a Healer	84
Letting Go	85
Breath as Connection	88

CHAPTER 7. THE SACRED MUNDANE … 92
    Filling the Bucket … 92
    The Stream … 93
    The Repetition … 95
    A Quiet Revelation … 96
    Moving Stones … 98
    A Shift … 100
    Finding Flow … 101
    Completing the Circle … 103
    Returning to the Water … 104
    Back to the Stones … 105
    The Revelation … 106
    A New Perspective … 108

CHAPTER 8. INTO THE CURRENT … 110
    The Reluctance … 110
    The Edge … 111
    The Push … 113
    The Lesson of the Ganga … 115
    The Illusion of Certainty … 117
    The Ripple Effect … 118

CHAPTER 9. THREE REALIZATIONS … 122
    The Unveiling of Ego … 122
    Ego as a Mask … 124

The Unveiling 126
Pain as a Path 127
The Lesson of the Flame 128
The Mirror of the Ganga 130
The Healing in Surrender 132
The Present Moment 132
Anchoring in the Present 135
A Moment of Surrender 136
A New Beginning 137

CHAPTER 10. A GLIMPSE OF INFINITY 139
The Threshold of the Infinite 139
Unlocking the Points 140
The 33 Energy Points Awakening 142
  1. The Coccyx and Sacrum – Stability 143
  2. The Lumbar Spine – Compassion 144
  3. The Lower Thoracic Spine - Discernment 144
  4. The Upper Thoracic Spine - Courage 145
  5. The Cervical Spine – Creation 146
  6. The Atlas – Introspection 147
A Glimpse of Something More 148
Surrendering to the Infinite 150
The Act of Surrender 151
The Breaking Point 153
The Symphony of Wisdom 154
Stability: The Unshakable Ground 155
Compassion: The Warmth of the Heart 156
Discernment: Seeing Through the Veil 156

Courage: The Fire Within 157
Introspection: Turning Inward 158
Creation: Manifesting the Flow 158
Surrender: Becoming the Flow 159
The Circle Completes 160
The Infinite Journey 163

CHAPTER 11. THE RIVER WITHIN 166
The River's Dual Nature 166
The Power of Adaptation 168
A Call to Trust 170
The Dance of Resilience 171
The Weight of Resistance 173
The Lesson of the Pebbles 173
Becoming Part of the Flow 175
The Harmony of Nature 176
The Whisper of the Infinite 177
The Symphony of Connection 178
The Flow Within 179
Returning to the River 180

CHAPTER 12. RETURNING HOME 184
The Silent Farewell 184
Packing the Intangible 185
The Final Teaching 186
A Moment of Stillness 187
Walking the Path Forward 189
The First Test of Patience 190

Final Conversation with Rudra ... 192
The Road Ahead ... 194
The Test of Trust ... 195
The Farewell ... 196
The First Act of Integration ... 197

CHAPTER 13. WALKING THE INNER JOURNEY ... 199
The Journey is Never Over ... 199
The Weight of Transition ... 200
The Flight Home ... 201
The First Night Back ... 203
The Ripples Begin ... 206
The Challenge of Integration ... 207
Sharing the Flow ... 208
Inspiring the Flow ... 209
The Power of Sharing ... 210
Moments of Doubt ... 211
The Infinite Flow ... 212
A Closing Prayer ... 213

Acknowledgments ... 215
To My Beloved Wife ... 215
To My Two Little Sons ... 216
To My Mother: The Source of Endless Love ... 217
To My Father: Strength and Wisdom Legacy ... 217
To My Friends: My Chosen Family ... 218
To My Mentor and Guru ... 219
To the Seven Monks ... 219

To Rudra	220
To the Mountains and the Ganga: My Silent Teachers	221
To You, the Reader	222
Appendix	**224**
Exercise / Process	225
1. The Breath: Your Anchor in the Storm	225
2. Gratitude: Shifting Your Perspective	225
3. The Art of Presence: Mindful Observation	226
4. Transforming the Mundane: Repetitive Task Practice	227
5. Embracing Dualities: Finding Balance	227
6. Nature as a Teacher: Reconnecting with the Earth	228
7. Rituals: Creating Meaningful Moments	228
A Final Thought	229
Bonus Gift for Readers	229

FOREWORD

There are different kinds of books—some are meant to entertain, some to educate, and then there are those rare ones that transcend both. They don't just inform or amuse; they transform. They reach beyond the pages and into the depths of our consciousness, shifting our perspective, expanding our understanding, and awakening something deep within. *The Silent Path: A Journey Within* is one such book. It isn't merely a collection of words—it is an experience. A gateway to an inner journey that beckons you to explore your infinite potential.

I still remember my deep conversation with Cherag. It was more than just an exchange of words—it was an insight into his soul. As we spoke, I could see him transitioning, shifting from the logic zone to the magic zone. His mind, always sharp and analytical, was now surrendering to something greater, something unseen yet deeply felt. Through this book, that transition is evident. It is his bridge between intellect and intuition, between reason and faith, between knowing and simply being.

Cherag's life experiences—his journey through loss, his spiritual quests, and the moments of profound stillness—have all converged into this book. It is a testament to the wisdom he has gathered, not through mere study but through lived experience. The loss of his best friend became a turning point, a catalyst that propelled him inward, searching for meaning beyond the tangible. His encounters with enlightened beings, his time spent in the stillness of the mountains, and his surrender to silence have all shaped the essence of *The Silent Path*.

This book arrives as a breath of fresh air in a world overwhelmed by noise. It does not demand your belief—it invites your presence. It does not dictate a path—it helps you find your own. As you journey through these pages, you will feel the presence of those guides who illuminated Cherag's way, not as abstract ideals but as practical wisdom, revealed in moments of quiet revelation. This book does not merely speak about transformation; it embodies it.

But here's the beautiful part: this book is not just about Cherag. It is about you. It is a mirror reflecting your untraveled roads, your unanswered questions, and your dormant wisdom waiting to be remembered. It gently nudges you to slow down, to breathe, to listen—not just to the words, but to the spaces between them, for that is where the real magic unfolds.

The greatest teachers do not stand above us; they walk beside us. And that is what Cherag does through this book. He does not claim to have all the answers, nor does he position himself as a guru. Instead, he becomes a companion, a fellow traveler on this path of awakening. With each page, he urges you to not just read but to *feel*. To not just understand, but to *experience*.

This is not a book you merely finish and put aside. It is one that lingers within you, reshaping your thoughts, shifting your emotions, and calling you back to yourself. It is a reminder that true peace isn't found in resistance, but in surrender—surrender to the natural rhythm of life, to the silent wisdom that has always been within you.

So, as you turn these pages, I urge you—let go. Let go of your need to control, to rationalize, to analyze. Let this book do what it was meant to do: move you, awaken you, transform you. Let it carve a path not just in your mind, but in your heart.

Cherag, this book is a gift—not just to those who seek, but to those who are ready to listen. And I have no doubt that it will find its way into the hands of those who need it most.

To your magical journey,

Siddharth Rajsekar

INTRODUCTION

There's always a way life shows its ugly face in the most unexpected moments. Every day, you think you know where you are; you're walking a path you've walked time and time again, secure in your feet; and then one day, the ground gives way, and it all crumbles. That's how my journey began—not with clarity or purpose, but with a loss so profound that it erased my sense of self and left me searching for answers I didn't even know how to ask.

The Subject of this book is about that **search**. A journey of Letting Go, Surrender, and Finding Strength.

It's not too much to say that losing my job might sound like a simple thing or one that happens. This was not only a job for me, it was who I was, it was how I navigated, the rhythm of my life. Without it, I felt spacey or as if the ground had vanished beneath me and left me hanging in a loud empty nothing.

You know which kind of fear I'm talking about; if you've ever stood at the edge of yourself, staring into the void. The questions came in like waves: *Who am I? What do I do now? How do I rebuild myself when I can't even focus on what I'm building?*

For the next few days, I wandered through that mental fog, staying occupied with the help of all of the distractions, trying to patch the gaps. But nothing worked. As if life was put on pause.

Then one night all of a sudden, I felt someone whisper the words "The Himalayas" and something shifted, a pull I cannot explain, it almost felt like a calling that I couldn't ignore.

The Himalayas had always been a source of wonder. The peaks felt mythical, almost sacred, as if they held secrets—secrets beyond explanation, beyond the reach of language. I had no idea what the calling was, or what it wanted from me. Was it the dream that I had in my younger days, a wish that was buried in the tasks of life resurfacing itself? I didn't have the answer, but I knew I had to trust my instinct, I had to answer this call.

The decision wasn't easy. Leaving my family, my responsibilities, and my comforts behind felt impossible. I shared my thoughts with my wife, Sabah, and she surprised me. She didn't argue about my wanting to go or plead with me not to. She looked at me with zero uncertainty and said, "Go. We'll be here." Those words felt like an anchor in my journey and a permission slip for taking my first step forward into the unknown.

I came to Rishikesh, carrying just a small bag and a heavy heart filled with questions and doubt. I knew from the moment I set foot on the sacred land that it was no longer a simple journey. This wasn't about how many miles I was about to walk or where I would be walking them. It was something more—to reckon, to rediscover, to find out who I really was.

And then, one evening, as the sun went down the horizon, I met a stranger. When I look back this meeting was one of those life's moments, so unremarkable, it ought never to have happened, except it did, and then everything changed. "You seem lost!" he said. This was not an accusation, nor a question. It felt as if the stranger was holding a mirror to my soul.

What followed was a journey so profound, I never thought it would turn out to be. Walking through the terrain of the Himalayas, tested me every step of the way both physically and mentally. I remember those nights having silence so deep that it reached inside me. Lessons that I did not expect to see unfold in stillness, repetition, and surrender.

The mountains disrobed me of my ego, my assumptions, of my phony need to control. It was not just my strength they had tested; they had reformed it. They revealed to me the truth of my life which I had been too afraid or too blind to see.

And then there was the river 'The Ganga,' a body of water powerful yet calm. It felt as if the river had a mind of its own exactly knowing where to flow. It felt the Ganga was ready to instruct me, teach me life lessons I wasn't prepared to learn. I will never forget the moment I found myself in the icy grasp of the river. My first instinct was to fight it. But there was no way the river was going to let me win. In that freezing, frantic moment, I discovered the most important life lesson: the power to surrender.

Don't think of surrender as a defeat, surrender is trust. Trust in life, in the flow of its existence, the notion that we don't have to have all the answers to move forward.

At that moment in the river, I had not reached the end of my journey; but it was just the beginning—a doorway into a new level of understanding, of myself and the world.

Introduction

As I left the mountains, I didn't leave the life lessons behind. They came with me and are still teaching me, showing me a path on how I live, how I see, and how I connect.

This book is not about the Himalayas, nor is it a step-by-step manual on enlightenment. It's an offering. A story. An invitation to hear the whispers of your soul. The path doesn't need mountains or rivers. It only asks for one thing: willingness to take that first step.

So, let's turn the page together as we walk this path. We'll go into the silence that speaks louder than words, the beauty of letting go, and the infinite possibilities that are open when we stop looking outside and start listening to the voice within.

With love and gratitude,

Cherag

CHAPTER 1

WEIGHT OF THE WORLD

At its core, life is an act of fine-balancing everything. We place titles, relationships, and achievements on top of each other and hope they will hold us. But, have you thought about what happens, when one of those pillars crumbles? It wasn't just crumbling for me; it was an implosion, and I was left standing in the ruins of my definition of me.

It all started with an email. A single line—detached and impersonal that altered my life: "*We regret informing you…*" I read it, and read it again, wishing that the words rearranged and their meaning changed. But they didn't. I had lost my job, my title, and at that moment, it felt like I had really lost my identity.

I'll ask you this: Do you know what it feels like to tie your identity to something external? It might be your job, your relationship, or a role you play for others. And when it's not there anymore, have you felt that deep panic? If you have, I think you'd know the void I was staring into. Let this be a reminder that you should explore who you really are, beyond the things, beyond the ropes that hold you from going too far.

I was in shock, angry, and not wanting to believe it. I wanted to call someone, anyone, and reached for my phone, only stopping myself. What would I even say? Maybe it's because I wasn't required anymore.

In the deafening silence of my home office, I sat there, staring at the screen. I replayed in my mind every project I had led, every late night I had spent burning the candle at both ends. Was it all meaningless? For me, my job was never just a job, it was my badge of honor, a mirror that says this was the version of myself I am proud of. Without it, who am I?

The Weight of Expectations

What followed was a void, as if everything had distanced itself into the haze. I filled my time with productive things—revising my resume, sending emails, and updating my LinkedIn profile. With every rejection email, I felt like a personal accusation — an announcement that I wasn't good enough. It wasn't right out there on the surface, but beneath all the distractions and disbelief something was brewing.

I had stopped looking in the mirror, a mirror that life was so desperate to show me no matter where I would hide. I was terrified of facing the question: *What happens when your achievements are taken away from you? Without the applause who are you?*

I grew up with the understanding that the world loves labels. Labels simplify things. "He's a CEO," or "She's an artist." However, what if your 'label' is taken away? It feels like free-falling into an identity vacuum.

On that evening; just after another day of trying to be busy and mind filled with self-doubt, I found Sabah, my wife, sitting right there with me, in our living room. She didn't ask me how I was, because she didn't have to. She could read from my body language, the slump of my shoulders, the way my eyes wouldn't meet hers, she understood something was wrong. Instead of drilling about what was wrong and asking me a million questions, she did something simple yet profound: She sat beside me, putting her hand on mine. And mumbled softly, "Talk to me."

But I couldn't. How can you talk about a pain so overwhelming it feels like you are being redefined by it? What do you tell the person you're closest to, the one you love the most, when you yourself are fading away?

Sabah didn't press. Her presence anchored me. In her presence, I allowed myself to breathe for the first time in the last few days.

I've learned that to breathe is to surrender. So, it's a reminder that life goes on, even during our darkest moments. In that silence, with nothing but my breath and Sabah's anchoring presence, a memory appeared.

As a child, I had grown up adoring those towering peaks called the Himalayas, and was always fascinated by their snow-capped summits. More than mountains, they were symbols of something more. Freedom. Stillness. Eternity.

I had pictured myself countless times standing at their bases, staring up at their enormity. Often in life, our fantasies get buried under practical considerations. School, work, family want to devour you, and you are left with little to no room for your dreams.

Sitting with this question of who I was, the Himalayas came back, as if the wind was carrying the whisper. At first, I dismissed it. What was I going to do in the mountains? Find answers? Look for redemption? Maybe a fresh start? It all seemed absurd. Yet, the thought persisted. Not loud, not forceful but steady. It was a quiet pull, an invisible pull at my heart, which almost felt like a life calling. I didn't know what to do with it, couldn't explain it, nor was I able to walk away from it.

Have you ever felt this before? Or perhaps just one of those peculiar calls that makes no sense. Something you feel you can't explain, but one you know you need to follow? If you have, you'll be able to empathize with that mix of fear and curiosity I felt. If you haven't, I hope this story inspires you to listen next time when those whispers come.

The First Step

I wrestled with the idea for the next few days. The rational part of me wanted to write it off because of every reason as to why it was impractical. What would I tell Sabah? What about my responsibilities? What if I didn't find anything in those mountains? And it's time to find the next job and not to go on the hunt of soul-searching

At the very least, the heart isn't logical. Every time I tried to suppress the thought it grew stronger. It wasn't a demand. It was an invitation. One that asked everything but promised nothing.

One evening, as Sabah and I sat in the living room, I finally shared my thoughts. I said "I think I need to go somewhere," barely above a whisper.

Her eyes searched mine; she looked at me and asked. "Where?"

"The Himalayas." I was bracing myself for her reaction. Would she laugh? Will she dismiss the idea as foolish? But she didn't. Instead, she asked the question I hadn't asked myself: "Why?"

No words came from my mouth as I tried to answer. How can I explain something I didn't completely understand? How do I tell her that the mountains are like both an escape and a homecoming?

"I don't know," I admitted. "I just feel like I need to go. Now, I have to step away from everything and figure out who I am now. Or who I am supposed to be"

Sabah didn't look away. She didn't question or even argue with this, "If that's what you need, then go," she said.

Reflection for the Reader

have you ever been in a situation where the person looks right through you? Leaving you with a feeling of being vulnerable. They see you for who you are instead of what you could do for them?

They were words of gift, of understanding, of trust. They made me remember there are times when the best love we can show someone is to give them room to discover themselves.

As I sat there, letting her words sink in, I realized something profound: I wanted more than the mountains. I was seeking me. All the personal versions of myself that lived beneath labels and expectations. The one version I had neglected for too long.

It wasn't an easy decision to make. Fear always hangs on, hissing at the reasons why it is a mistake. I could feel the fear that filled my body, but with it, there was something else—some tiny spark of hope. Maybe, just maybe, this trip would lead me back to myself.

As I thought about the idea to go, it didn't lift the weight of the world off my shoulders. It was heavy and unrelenting. But I felt strong enough to carry it. I didn't have answers, but I was willing to go find them.

This first step was not into the mountains, but into my life, into the unknown—into what fear feels like and how it can be broken so that the gift of transformation can enter.

Deciding to leave for the Himalayas was one thing; doing it was another. Those days were a cinch of hustle, bustle, and emotion. On the outside, it was pretty good and exciting, but beneath the surface, there was this quiet storm of fear, doubt, and anticipation.

When I sat down with Sabah to share all the details (or lack thereof) of what I was planning. "I don't know where I'll be or for how long," I said. "I have to move, that's all I know."

She gave me a nod while she spoke softly, but her silence told more. She didn't need to reassure me or have a debate. It was something that only someone who deeply loves you would comprehend. She finally said "You've been holding your breath for too long. Maybe it's time to just flow."

I could hear her words resonating in my mind, dropping them like a ship's anchor. The truth was, she was right. I had been holding my breath not for days or weeks, but years. I had always tried; I had always worked to be rewarded; for being acknowledged; and I felt like I carried a lot of expectations. Her assurance felt like a glimmer of freedom.

Packing More Than a Bag

It wasn't just packing the necessary clothes and supplies for a journey like this. It was about making a choice: what parts of my old life would I take with me — what could I leave behind?

I took out an old backpack, its worn fabric souls me of past adventures I had wanted to have, but never did. Inside, I packed the essentials: The idea was to take very few sets of clothes, a journal, a pen, and a small picture of my family.

One of my favorite photographs is the one, taken a few months back during my kids' 2nd birthday. My two boys Arhum and Aarish are smiling from ear to ear, ice cream all over their faces. Sabah's laughter freezes in place and stands beside them.

Holding the photo, I feel guilty. What kind of father runs away to pursue a calling he can't even see, a calling that doesn't guarantee anything? Would they understand? Would they forgive me?

The photograph went into a side pocket of my bag that was close enough to touch but out of sight. So, of course, it wasn't just a reminder of what I was leaving behind, it was a promise to return—physically, yes, but also as a better version of myself.

Conversations with Myself

The night before I was leaving, the house was quiet and soft and I sat alone in the living room. Out there in the world, it was dark, everyone else was asleep.

My mind raced in the stillness. What if all this is for nothing? And what if I come back lost? Then more lost than I am now?

We're most vulnerable when fear creeps in. It whispers doubts and it sows uncertainty. But as I sat there, looking into the shades, a bit of voice came over, perhaps a little quieter and steadier. *But what if this is exactly what you need?*

Which felt like a lifeline — these questions pulled me from the spiral of doubt. This reminded me it wasn't about whether I was going to achieve something or not and also not having that guarantee. Taking that step forward while trusting the process, even though you don't know exactly where it is heading.

Into the quiet, I whispered, a promise to myself that, "I don't know what lies ahead. But I will show up. I will confront whatever comes my way, not as the person I believe I should be, but as the person I am."

The Departure

Gently dawn broke, the first rays of the sun spilling in through the windows as I gathered my things. Fear did not hold me back; it was a purpose.

I met Sabah's eyes with a mixture of pride and worry. She took me into a hug, saying: "Take care of yourself. And remember you are never really alone."

Stepping outside the cool morning air brushed against my skin, her words, which had occupied me from the moment she had told them, stayed with me. One last look I gave the house, and the life I was leaving behind, and faced the horizon.

The drive up to the airport was in silence; the only sound was that coming from the hum of the car. I could hear Mumbai's chaotic rhythm pulled with horns blaring, life up and running. Nevertheless, at that moment, the city and I existed in two worlds. The city thrived in its familiar chaos while I was stepping away to become unknown.

The world blurred past and the car weaved through the traffic as I stared out the window. And the neon-lit streets of Mumbai, the overcrowded crossroads, the continuous honking, started to fade away. I was untethered for the first time in years, not in a scary sense, but a freeing one, as if I was peeling it off my back, it was something I no longer needed.

I came to the airport, stopped, and stood at the entrance of the airport for a moment, holding my bag on my shoulder. This was the destination: no return. A part of me started to wonder if I should turn back, in retreat from the familiar, into the safe. That is, until I thought of the mountains and the quiet whisper that had brought me here. Heaving out a sigh, I readjusted my bag and walked through the glass doors.

I had a blend of emotions when the plane rose up through the skies. Relief. Anticipation. And, yes, fear. However, there was something new along with it all, a spark of hope.

The clouds covered Mumbai, and its expansive land turned into a crisscross of lights and shadows. Looking from this height, I saw how tiny the city was, and with it, how tiny my problems seemed. Perspective can raise you above the noise and make us remember that life is bigger than the stories we tell ourselves.

Although the hum of the plane's engines would be disturbing, that day they were a sort of white noise that lulled me into a meditative state. I closed my eyes and allowed my mind to wander away. I remember the moments of joy, the moments of togetherness with Sabah, the boys around the dinner table, the rush to work. All memories came in a flash. Soon turning into a blur, like a reel of film going on fast forward.

Somewhere in that haze of memories, I felt the weight of what I was leaving behind: my family and responsibilities along with the identity I had clung to for so long. Rather than regret there was this odd sense of liberation.

Have you ever felt that? The instance when you recognize that surrender doesn't imply misfortune — it is whatever else!

The crisp cool air of the foothills welcomed me when the plane landed in Dehradun. Such a stark difference to Mumbai's humid hold, I breathed it in deeply and felt the clarity of it settling over me.

The airport was small, almost quaint, and wasn't busy either. I picked up my bag and went outside where a cab was waiting to take me to Rishikesh.

The drive from Dehradun airport to Rishikesh was an entry to a different world. Then the scenery began to change as the cab wound its way through the roads. In a short while, the dense urban sprawl receded to give way to open fields, then more greenery, and eventually the majestic hills having the gateway to the Himalayas.

The driver was a kind man with a warm smile, he started chatting with me briefly before falling into a companionable silence. It was good, this quiet was good; exactly what I needed. An earth and leaves scent wafted in with the cool breeze, as I rolled down the car window.

Now and then the Ganga would sweep into view, flashing its liquid silver ribbon as the sun struck it. Its presence felt calming, almost magnetic. I was immediately drawn to its flow, its serenity. It echoed something inside of me that felt the same, this quiet chaos and steady drumbeat on the surface.

> ## Reflection for the Reader
>
> *Do you know how nature has a gift for keeping you grounded? What reminds you of life's simplicity buried under those complexities? As I watched the river flow alongside the road, I couldn't help but wonder: Do we take the time to listen to the whispers of the world around us as much as we should?*
>
> *Life moves fast. And then before you know it, we're caught up in it, the noise from the city's buzzes, responsibility piles up. But what if we paused? What if we would allow ourselves to sit in the stillness and let it see what it is in front of us?*

The Arrival in Rishikesh

It was more than that, Rishikesh was not just a physical part of the journey, it was also an emotional, and essentially spiritual pilgrimage. Every mile was another layer, another turn, another step, closer to something I couldn't yet define.

There were people everywhere, and, all of a sudden Rishikesh felt like a different dimension in which I had stepped. A vibrancy different from the bustle of anywhere else, yet calm and serene. The streets held the pilgrims and travelers, their faces had the same blend of curiosity as that on mine.

Flowing through the heart of the town, the Ganga looked as tempting close up as it did from afar. It drew people to its banks; some officiated rituals, others sat quietly in awe.

I was staying at a small guest house overlooking the river. An elderly innkeeper with a smile, and a grin, handed me the key to my room. He pointed to the hotel balcony: "The Ganga" He continued, "You see, she takes care of everyone who comes here." My room was small but comfortable, its windows facing the Ganga. I stood there, absorbing it all while feeling a peace I hadn't felt in years.

The evening, when the sun went below the horizon, I wandered towards the riverbank. I drew myself towards the crowd, the famous Ganga Aarti was about to start near Triveni Ghat.

It was a symphony of sight, sound, and scent; flickering oil lamps in the twilight, rising chants into the air, incense smelling the breeze. Standing at the edge of the banks I watched the beauty of the ritual. It seemed as if the whole town united, people chanting in devotion to celebrate the river for its vital life-supporting role.

At that moment, I heard it: that whisper, again. The whisper that had guided me here was the same. This time it wasn't just a sound. Not just a calling, it was a feeling—a knowing.

When I got back to my guesthouse that evening, my mind was, strangely, quiet. No swirling thoughts, no nagging doubts – just the steady rhythm, like the river outside my window.

This was the first time I let myself truly be a part of the journey I was on. I didn't have all the answers, and it didn't matter or know what was ahead. I had done something, that was all that mattered.

Reflection for the Reader

How would you begin? What would happen if you placed fear and doubt aside, what journey could you take?

CHAPTER 2

RIVER'S CALL

Selfie at the river near Rishikesh... On reflection, the road into Rishikesh was like walking into the pages of a long-lost story, a place I had never been but I felt I had always known. The air began to stretch as it went colder, and lighter, carrying an indescribable energy. They changed the atmosphere, the rhythm of their life, and the feeling in my chest, not just the geography.

In books I had read about Rishikesh and in conversations with travelers, it was called the spiritual gateway to the Himalayas. No description would have prepared me for the way Ganga flows through the heart of the town. Its waters shifted between jade and silver in the encounter with sunlight. It wasn't a river, not a mere river, it was a presence, a living, full presence that pulsed with ancient wisdom.

Rishikesh is a place covered with hot and cold contrasts. It hums on one hand with the temples all ringing with the sound of bells, the streets on another all busy and narrow with merchants selling you trinkets and spices, and raving in a dozen different languages. However, it radiates serenity. Deep in the heart of chaos lies a rhythm as old and unshakeable as the town itself seems to breathe in sync with the river.

I walked through the streets that afternoon and saw that the locals were unhurried as if time was a different affair. Sadhu saints clad in saffron robes sat in quiet meditation near temple steps. I sat down in a tea stall looking over the river. A young man with bright eyes, (at the tea stall) served me a steamed cup of chai. He asked, "First time in Rishikesh?" The way he said it was friendly.

"Yes," I replied. He pointed to the path towards the river bank and said, "Then you must sit by the Ganga. She can clear one's head." He spoke as if I'm being guided by a divine universal message, and I walked the path; the sound of rushing water getting louder and louder.

The First Encounter

The waters of the river moved in a way as that was the only sound on the riverbank. I sat down cross legged, under a tree with my cup of tea. The serene Ganga stretched out in all her glory, her current unrelenting but steady. Her waters flowed over the rocks, around bends and through obstacles, carving her path with a grace that seemed easy and almost effortless.

I remember, as I sat there, a memory from years ago… When I was just a child. I had read about the Ganga, about how she was much more than just a river. She was a goddess, a force of transformation, a nurturer. Travelers who travelled thousands of miles, came to bathe in her waters inferring they could cleanse their sins and find clarity.

As I sat there, I believed the truth of those stories of legends. The river Ganga was not just a river: it was a mirror. A mirror that showed not just the world around her, but that spiraled into the inner world of anyone who looked.

As I watched the river, I allowed its rhythm to wash over me. This was the first day my thoughts had settled since the day I left Mumbai.

> ### Reflection for the readers
>
> *Have you ever felt that? It's a moment when the noise in your head goes away and there's room for something a little quieter, something more profound?*

The sun started to go down, painting the water with the most beautiful shade of gold, and I remembered what I've been holding on to: grief, doubt, fear. The loss of my job had shaken me, yes, but it had also forced me to confront the truth: So, I had built my identity around things that could be taken: titles, accomplishments, security. On the other hand, Ganga, with her endless flow, asked a simple question: *Who are you without all that?*

I didn't have an answer. Not yet. Yet, I was alright with that. The river didn't ask questions, it let me sit, listen, and just be.

That evening as I made my way back to the guesthouse the town had almost become silent. Bells from the temples were ringing off in the distance and the smell of incense filled the air. I felt a bit of my burden Ganga had carried away with her current, and I felt a strange sense of peace.

That night as I lay in my bed, I was thinking about the pull that had brought me here. I know it wasn't logical or rational but it was so real. For, I didn't feel the need to resist. It was just the tip of the iceberg. I knew I didn't know what was coming next, but I had a strong feeling that I was exactly where I was supposed to be.

Reflection To the Reader

Have you ever stood on the brink of something which is greater than you? Was it something that made you doubt everything you believed you knew?

If that's the case, then you know how much courage it takes to step forward. If you've already found the call, I hope this story makes you remember the call is always there, no matter what, waiting for you to listen to it.

The river flows. The mountains rise. This is your most authentic self, my friend, and somewhere in between it lies the path.

In the morning, light began slowly cascading through misty trees as if it were softly painting a delicate painting, a canvas drenched in golden soft light. Slowly the town would wake, the step with the river. Temple bells hummed in the distance merged with the sounds of the morning chants and the soft sound of the Ganga.

I stepped out from my guesthouse onto a narrow street that led into the river bank to explore more of this sacred town. It was still, the air broken sporadically by the sound of chirping birds.

It was not an emptiness, the silence was presence, as if the whole town was always in a state of meditation.

Rishikesh wasn't just anywhere, it was a doorstep to something holy, something more. It was as if the town existed in two dimensions simultaneously: ***the earthly and the divine.***

The Ganga Aarti

However, that evening I went over to Triveni Ghat; it is a very sacred site. The Ghat was buzzing with activities; pilgrims collecting the best offerings of flowers and diyas, families sitting together on the stairs, and travelers like me, trying to find something that we could not put a name on.

The atmosphere changed as the sun set. Priests clad in traditional attire took charge of the Ganga Aarti, a prayer held in worship of the river's water, and the air filled with a sense of anticipation.

High upon the rooftops, the golden flames of lamps danced in the twilight on each as the ceremony began. There were priests on the edge of the river holding their large brass aartis from which spirals of fragrant smoke rose. Their movements synchronized; it was a dance of devotion that appeared to be beyond the physical world.

And then it was on, Sanskrit chants that made the earth steady. I didn't understand all the words, but I could feel the power. They seemed to be magnified with the joint prayers of each person there, stitching them into a rich, layered, and threadbare honor of surrender.

I knew I had to see the river glow with the light of thousands of floating diyas, and an inexplicable pull of some kind gripped my heart. The Ganga was not a river but a Goddess, a life giver and she had wounds, like all living things.

Have you ever had a moment in which time stopped, and everything around you felt both massive and close? The Aarti felt like that—that it was eternal and that every person there was connected to each other and to something much larger than them.

I stayed beside the river after the Aarti, I couldn't tear myself away. The crowd had thinned and I found a relatively quiet spot to sit on the steps with my feet so close to the water. It was gentle and unyielding, the Ganga's current, its surface flickering light of the diyas now floating further downstream.

I thought to myself that I had left behind my job and my family, my life. It sat heavy on my chest, it pressed on, and then my mind started to wonder why I had come here. What was I hoping to find? Answers? Clarity? Redemption?

River sensed my blues. Her waters lapped against the steps, rhythmic and soothing, as though she was whispering: "Let go."

Let go. It was an impossibly tricky phrase to say, yet so simple. How do you release what has become a part of who you are? If you want to release the identity you've clung to for so long, then how?

I sat there and I knew that letting go isn't about forgiving or forgetting to let your past go. It was about accepting it... Really, making peace with it in order to create space for something new.

The encounter with the stranger

After the night had gotten deeper, I saw a figure leaning a few feet from me, his shadow made with the soft light of the moon. He was tall and his frame lean but firm and he stood motionless, joining the flow of the river.

I didn't know him before, but there was something about him, something like a thread in the fabric of my journey that was now visible.

He looked up at me and walked in my direction. He moved, deliberately, unhurried, but purposeful. His voice was calm, steady, and accented by years in many places when he spoke. He pointed to the river, "You heard her call, didn't you?"

His question took me off guard but I nodded, I honestly wasn't sure what to say.

"But not everyone listens," he continued, "she speaks to everyone. Are you here because you heard her?"

I wanted to ask him how he knew all this but he was disarming. It didn't feel like he was a stranger. He was someone that had been waiting for this moment, this conversation.

"Yes," I said. "I heard her."

He smiled faintly, confirming something that he already knew. He said the Ganga doesn't just flow through the land — it is the land. "She flows through you. Through all of us. She's not asking for worship and she's not asking you to repent, she's asking you to surrender."

Surrender. There was that word again. With his gaze on the water, he sat down beside me. We sat for a while in silence that wasn't awkward or forced, it felt like he was waiting for me to ask the questions I didn't even know I had.

Finally, I broke the silence. "So, what does it mean to surrender?"

He looked at me thoughtfully. "It means stopping to fight the current," he said. "…to trust the river knows where she's taking you, even if you don't."

His words touched a chord inside of me. I had spent so much of my life fighting: fighting to win, to return to what I had been told I had to be. All my efforts only drove me further away from the person I was. And yet here I was, by this ancient river.

He added, as if he could telepathically hear my thoughts, "Surrender isn't weakness. It's one thing to let go of what isn't yours anymore; but, to let go of things that are no longer useful, so that you may ride the wave of what is."

> ## Reflection for the readers
>
> It wouldn't let me rest that night, as I walked back to the guesthouse after his words. It wasn't about giving up; it was about giving in. Defeat not too, but to something greater than yourself.
>
> Have you ever felt that pull? Or the call to stop hanging on, to stop fighting, to simply allow yourself to be taken by the current?
>
> It's terrifying, isn't it? To trust in something that you have no control over, to step out in the unknown, without a map or plan to follow. But it's also liberating. When you surrender you no longer fight the world, you ally with it.
>
> That night, as I lay in my bed, staring up at the ceiling, I had a weird kind of peace. I didn't have answers—not yet—but I had a question that felt far more important: What if the river was right? What if the way to finding myself wasn't by holding on but by letting go?

The Ganga had called me to Rishikesh, but it wasn't the worship or devotion she was asking for. She was asking for trust. In that moment, I felt ready.

As I packed my bag for the day ahead the morning light spilled across the room. I had booked a Sherpa (mountain guide) to guide me into the deeper part of the mountains and that was the last Sherpa at the camp for the season, so my plan was to meet him. However, life is never how you plan it to be.

The Unexpected News

I was at a small café next to the river, drinking hot ginger tea, and my phone buzzed. The Sherpa had sent a message. *"I'm sorry but I won't be able to lead you on this trek. My family is having an emergency and I need to get back home. I'm sorry for your inconvenience."*

Feeling confused, I reread the message in hopes it hadn't gone as I picked it up from it. I let the words settle, and my heart sank. What now?

I had flown from Mumbai, arranged for a cab to Rishikesh, absorbed the spiritual vibes of the town, and, all this while believing that it had a purpose. Suddenly it felt like the ground had been pulled out from under me. My mind raced with questions. Should I find another guide? Should I head back to Mumbai? Was this a sign that I wasn't supposed to keep going?

I sat for a bit, frozen at a café, staring vaguely at the river beyond the window. But there was the Ganga, flowing on, indifferent to my fate, still as unabated as the mightiest river in this world.

I couldn't help but feel the irony. I was here trying to surrender, trying to trust, and the second I was asked to let go of control, I was already breaking down.

> ### Reflection for the readers
>
> *Have you ever felt that? The suffocating weight of uncertainty, the choking understanding that the universe's plans were fraying and you were lost.*

My thoughts started churning on self-doubt. Maybe this all was a mistake. Maybe I had to fact-check that I am ready enough for this journey. Perhaps I had heard the call wrong.

Those thoughts for sure had consumed me, but a quieter voice had other ideas. Wasn't the point of the journey this? To step into the unknown? Even when things didn't feel like they were going my way, how to trust in the development of events …

The Decision to Stay

I took a deep breath and looked out at the river. Her waters didn't flow because of obstacles or detours. She changed her ways, heights over boulders, creating new tracks when the old no longer got her anywhere. Maybe that was what I actually needed to do, **adapt**.

I decided to stay. I didn't know what my next step would be but I decided to allow the day to unfold and whatever it is, I would follow it.

I spent the rest of the day walking aimlessly through Rishikesh, letting my feet inform the flats where my body should be. It was vibrant but serene at the same time, the narrow lanes that made up the town comforting and the bright colors lightening the atmosphere. Groups of people meditated in silence and their faces had a calm glow. I have crossed the suspension bridge swaying a little with the gentle breeze. As I stood on the bridge it gave a beautiful view of the Ganga and her waters glittering in the midday sun. I sat on the railing out there for a while, allowing the river's magical energy to enter inside me. As I took each step, I felt a little bit lighter, as if the doing was letting my doubts loose.

As the day passed and grew into the evening, I again lay out on the river bank. It was still light, but softer and golden on the water. On the steps, I sat watching the current take the leaves and flowers downstream.

I wasn't alone for long. I saw out of the corner of my eye the figure of the stranger I had met the night before. His calm presence loosened my nerves from the get go and he approached with the same unhurried pace. He sat down beside me, without invitation, and said, "You look troubled."

For a moment, I hesitated. Should I tell him that the trek was canceled? Would he understand that the biggest mistake I ever made was being disappointed in him? But there was something about him, however, that invited honesty.

"I had my guide cancel," I admitted with a heaviness flaming down into my voice. "I don't know what to do now. I came all this way and everything is falling apart."

His expression considered; he listened quietly. He nodded, as if he had heard this story, a thousand times before. "Do you know what the river teaches us?" he asked, pointing to the Ganga.

I shook my head. "We often don't know what the path is supposed to be," he said. "It twists and turns sometimes," continuing he said "Occasionally, it branches into smaller streams, or goes underground. However, the river always flows. The path isn't perfect, but she doesn't stop. She finds a way."

His words stilled over me like a balm. I felt my frustration begin to dissolve. "Starting to get it," I said, "I don't know how to get my way." He shrugged simply, "You don't have to know. All we need to do is take the next step."

An Invitation

He paused to give me a look, and then he said, "I'll lead the way. Then, if you're willing to trust the journey, I'll take you where you need to go."

That was an offer I hadn't been expecting. I had met him barely, this man of all men, as though he was here to be, here to meet me, as a piece of the river's design.

I know he wasn't just offering guidance, there was something in his eyes. He was providing understanding and a way to proceed not only through the mountains but also through the haze that was still inside of me.

Reflection for the Reader

Have you reached a fork in the road that you don't know which way to go? Do you ever feel your own expectations weighing in on the stream of living?

> *Those are moments where it's very easy to feel lost where you feel you've failed at everything. But what if it's not? So maybe those detours aren't detours. Maybe they're the journey themselves, the things that form us that we haven't seen yet.*

As I sat by the river that evening, listening to the stranger's calm voice, I realized something important: It's not about knowing where you're going. Trusting that every next step. But, my mind has a thousand questions: *Will it really get me closer to where I need to be? What then?* And then the quieter voice in my head said "Taking those steps no matter how uncertain is all that matters."

So, as the sun went down in Rishikesh, I made my choice. I would trust him. I would trust the river. And most importantly I would also trust myself. The mountains were calling and I answered. Ready or not. I just wasn't sure what lied ahead, I was ready to take the next step.

CHAPTER 3

THE TREK WITHIN

It was cool, and crisp, early morning air in Rishikesh, a kind of coolness that made me think of the untamed wilderness of the mountains just beyond. Within the bustling town, prayer bells and chai stalls were weaving between residents and visitors stirring to life. I found myself at the Ganga, watching its waters hurriedly and earnestly flow by. I didn't know where we were going, but the river did.

Standing a few steps behind me was the stranger still nameless in my mind. He was quiet, grounding, and enigmatic. His offer to guide me that previous evening had surprised me but as I now looked at the Ganga I had grown to love, I didn't want to turn back.

The night before, his voice was calm but firm when he'd said, "We leave at dawn."

It was the sun barely peeking over the horizon, my small backpack slung over my shoulders, and a thousand unanswered questions in my mind, and here we were.

The First Steps

Most treks begin on a well-trodden path out of town and this one was no exception. We made our way, the hum of Rishikesh was replaced by the rustling leaves, a chirp of a bird now and then. The ease with which my guide, the stranger, walked made me envy him. His steps were steady, purposeful, like he had walked this path numerous times before.

However, I was fighting my own pain, with my own thoughts and not just the physicality of walking. The backpack I was carrying started to feel heavier with every next step.

I asked, breaking the silence after what felt like forever, "Are you always this quiet?"

He turned, a slight smile and said: "The mountains don't speak in words. They speak in silence. You'll hear everything you need to know if you listen very closely."

I wasn't expecting that as the answer, but it silenced the churning in my mind.

The path headed up, into densely wooded hills and rocky land. With the midday sun up and the cool morning air no longer overlaying it, climbing here was even more grueling. A hurting ache spread through my legs, and sweat slowly dripped down my back.

"Why does this feel so hard?" Under my breath, I muttered, perhaps more to myself than to him.

"Because you're fighting it," he said, forcing my frustration to break through his voice. My breath was heavy, so I stopped and asked. "Fighting what?"

"Everything," he said. "The path. The climb. Your own thoughts."

There was something in his words, even though I wasn't ready to admit it.

Time spent away from the physical world was one thing, But, the fact that I felt like a failure could not be described in words, and then the continuous chatter in my brain which was relentless. *What if I can't do this? What if I've made a mistake?*

My every step carried thoughts that felt like large boulders. And I finally realized that I wasn't just climbing a mountain, that I was carrying the weight of my own expectations, of my own fear, of my own self-doubt.

Suddenly the stranger said, as if he could hear my thoughts, "Let it go."

"Let what go?" I asked, infuriated.

He stopped, staring at me. "The need to control. The need to know. We all have had an innate need to be something other than what we are at this moment."

I didn't have a response. How do you argue with something so clear it slices past you? Finally, the trail took us to a small clearing, in which the Ganga was briefly visible again with her waters shining in the light. The sight of her, soothing both my hurting legs as well as the turmoil in my mind.

"Why does the river feel so... alive?" I broke the silence and asked.

The stranger answered, "Because she is. The Ganga isn't just water. She's a force. A teacher. A guide."

I watched the river flow, her current steady and unyielding, his words sitting firm in the air. It hit me then, the Ganga wasn't just an accompaniment to this journey, it was a piece of the journey itself – a symbol for the flow I didn't want to surrender to.

He gestured pointing toward the river. "Then why does she never stop?" he asked.

I shrugged, not knowing how to answer. "Because she trusts. She doesn't fight the rocks or the bends in her path. She flows with them instead of against them. That's her strength."

The First Breakthrough

So, we sat by the riverside, the sound of water filled the silence between us. I remembered what he said about trust and surrender.

> ### Reflection for the readers
>
> *Have you ever struggled just to keep on pace or get ahead, only to find that you were swimming against the current, to attempt to control something that was never meant to be controlled in the first place?*

And then I sat there, and I realized, I had spent my whole life fighting to prove myself, fighting to fit into roles, fighting to hold onto things that were never mine.

The Ganga was flowing smoothly and was showing me how to let go.

Upon resuming the trek, I felt a gentle transformation in me. I wouldn't say that the climb was easier, but my resistance faded. I stopped looking at how far away we were and started looking at the next step, the next breath, the next moment.

The stranger nodded at me approvingly as he glanced back toward me. "Better." I didn't ask how he knew. Somehow, it didn't matter.

Reflection for the Reader

When I climbed that mountain one thing hit me: it's not just that you get to the mountain's top. It's about the journey, the lessons learned in the journey. Many times, we focus so much on the destination that we neglect to realize the path. All caught up in our own expectations that we can overlook the beauty of what is blooming right before us?

And if you have, you're not alone. We all do it. But what if we didn't? Imagine what we could do if we were willing to trust the process, and let life be, instead of fighting against it.

When the first part of the trek was coming to an end, I felt calm and a relief I hadn't felt in years. I wasn't the one spouting all the answers. I didn't know what lay ahead. And I was okay with that.

Into the Unknown

The further we climbed the thinner the air became and the lush greenery of the foothills gave way to rocky outcrops and ill-looking scrubland. Streams cut through the landscape, with only the occasional trickle where the Ganga had pushed her way out of sight, her rushing waters replaced. My legs hurt, my breath was short, but my unrelenting storm of thought was starting to quiet.

My guide, the stranger, proceeded ahead of me walking with purpose, but unhurried. It was comforting and challenging because he didn't talk and I had to listen to that loudness inside of me.

The trail became less defined, as we climbed higher, oftentimes just wandering over boulders and steep inclines. It was as uncertain, as unsure a path as my own journey. The stranger, however, without uttering a word would stop and look back to make sure I was following him.

"Do you ever get lost?" My voice penetrated the silence.

His expression calm, he turned. "You're not lost to the mountains. In the mountains, you always lose yourself," he added. I frowned, kind of annoyed and kind of intrigued at his cryptic comment. "And what does that mean?"

He simply shrugged. "Keep walking. You'll understand."

Part of me wanted to hunt for clarity, to demand answers. His presence, though, somehow, did not produce a sense of fear; it was there, though, with the quiet confidence that carried him. The silence between us was heavy but not oppressive. The silences were the same as the land around us vast and untamed with secrets.

> ### Reflection to the readers
>
> *Ever observed how when you're quiet you increase the depth of your introspect? Does it make you confront something that you've tried to avoid?*

The further into the wilderness we trekked, I started thinking about how the world I left behind used to be. How far away the titles were, the accolades, the constant push for more, they seemed so irrelevant compared to the scale of these mountains.

The stranger asked suddenly, startling me out of my thoughts, "What are you thinking about?"

"Everything," I admitted. "And nothing, all at once."

He nodded as if that all made perfect sense. "Good. You're starting to listen."

My expression was confused "To what?" He said simply, "To yourself."

The Steeper Path

The path forward tapered into two directions, one twisting sharply upward and the other bending softly around the roots of a hill. He stopped and looked between the two options.

"Which way?" Asking him, I expected him to know.

He countered, his eyes still staring at me, "Which way do you think?"

I hesitated, unsure. The incline promised it was to be a grueling climb up the steeper path. The other path seemed more inviting, almost too easy, the gentler path.

"Do we want to go higher?" I turned the decision over to him and asked.

He had a steady and calm face. "This isn't about me. It's about you. Which path feels right?"

Frustrated by his insistence on forcing me to choose, I sighed. But as I stood there, weighing my options, I realized something: The easy path doesn't usually bring about growth. I gave a deep breath and pointed to the trail which was steeper.

"Good," he said with a nod. "Now, let's see if you trust yourself enough to follow through."

Each step was more brutal than the one before it. My legs had turned to fire, my lungs sucked hollow and my mind oscillated from resolution to doubt.

I made the wrong choice, didn't I? What if I can't do this?

It was a steady pace, not rushed, but the stranger walked ahead. He didn't tell me to keep going or offer some sort of advice or encouragement, but his presence was enough to push me along.

"Why didn't you say which way to go?" Between labored breaths, I asked.

He didn't turn around to answer but he said, "It's not my journey. It's yours."

Every step up, his words lingered with me, as their truth settled in. How many times had I needed someone to direct me? Tell me what to do? To make sure my choices were acceptable? It was my moment; it was my path—challenges and all—including the struggle.

I stumbled about halfway up the incline, my foot getting caught on a loose rock. The impact on me was jarring, but not painful, I fell to my knees.

The stranger turned to look at me and stopped. "Are you hurt?"

I muttered "no" then, and proceeded to brush the dirt off my hands. "Just clumsy."

I paused before reaching out and taking his outstretched hand. He held my grip firmly, his pull in a steady motion as he helped me back to my feet.

Almost conversational, he asked, "Do you know what makes the mountain strong?"

I didn't know if he was serious, shaking my head. He said, "They don't fight the elements. The wind shapes them and the rain carves their bodies and the sun weathers them. What makes them strong is their endurance."

Nodding, I had no clue what to say. He was like a lesson, his words, words I wasn't ready to hear just yet but I couldn't get past them.

A Moment of Pause

A small plateau, a natural point of rest, with a view so breathtaking you wanted to stay lying there, forever. It was the time the great sun started going down, pushing the colors of gold and amber onto the landscape.

With a wave for me to do the same, the stranger sat down on a flat rock.

He broke the silence, "Why did you come here?"

I replied automatically, "To find something."

"What do you hope to find?" he asked.

The question caught me by surprise and I hesitated. "I don't know," I admitted.

He gave the faintest smile and said "Good. Our first step to understanding is to know we don't."

I gazed out over the valley, almost too beautiful, his words stayed in the air. I hadn't found any answers since the trek had started, but I was beginning to let go of the need to find them.

Reflection for the Reader

Have you ever gotten yourself to one of those crossroads and you don't know what to do? Have you ever crumbled underneath the weight of your own expectations of yourself, or felt the pressure to make the 'right' choice, to achieve the best?

If you have, know this: there is no perfect path. All you know is the one you decide to take. You learn something about yourself with every step, easy or difficult.

I became aware of this when I was sitting on that plateau and looking down at the mountains, the tops of which I had just arrived — that wasn't the journey. The journey was all about the climb, the struggles, the little moments of doubt, and the quiet victories along the way.

Sometimes, the most earth-shattering lessons can't be found within the answers, they are found within the questions we choose to ask. With that in mind, I stood up and continued my trek into the unknown.

CHAPTER 4

SILENCE AS A TEACHER

As we went on, the mountains fell silent, their towering shapes dropping shadows over the rock. The landscape by now almost felt like it was from another world, extending vast plains of stone and sky, with the occasional green tinted streak to mark stubborn plants stubbornly defying the harsh environment. Yes, beautiful, but also entirely isolating. In some ways, it was at that isolation that one begins to weave their spell of silence.

The Noise Within

That stranger—unknown and enigmatic, in nature, purpose—walked ahead, his steps sure and confident. Hours and hours went on since we had spoken but it wasn't avoidance. It felt on purpose like the silence was louder than the words. First, I filled the void with my thoughts, a merciless storm of worries and memories that wouldn't shut up. Hours turned to days, and something started to change.

Silence can make you strip down the layers of protection you created. Without the distractions, you are left with nothing else but your own thoughts and for me they were loud.

Do you ever notice your head chewing on noise? I think there's a hum of plans, regrets, what-ifs, just trying to keep you from the unknown. But here in the mountains, there was no net.

Every fear I had pushed aside came rushing forward: Was I wasting my time? What if this journey ended without any result? What if I couldn't find the answers I was looking for?

And then there was the guilt. I thought of Sabah, the life I had left behind, and my boys. Was I being selfish? Was this journey, after all, more of an escape, or was it actually leading toward something else?

The harder I tried to ignore these thoughts the louder they became. Somehow, as if speaking for themselves, the mountains themselves were making them louder, forcing me to confront what I had avoided for so long.

A Lesson from Nature

Another afternoon we stopped beside a clearing barely large enough to let us spread a blanket in the dry grass, where a small stream trickled over smooth stones. With cupped hands, the stranger knelt by the water, and drank. I didn't know whether to go with him or to stay away from him.

Suddenly his voice broke the hours-long silence. "Do you see the water?" he asked.

I nodded, confused. "Of course."

"Watch it," he said.

I crouched beside him following the stream as it meandered by the rocks. It wasn't rushing, or stagnant: it was flowing, tending to every obstacle in its path with soft grace.

"Do you suppose the water struggles?" he asked.

I frowned. "Struggles? It's just water."

His eyes as calm as the stream, he looked at me and said, "Exactly. It doesn't resist. It doesn't matter. It moves with what is."

His words saluted the water, and I stared at it, his words sunk in. Was I like that stream, flowing with life's currents? Or was I the rock, clinging, resisting as I held my ground?

The Language of Silence

The way we were walking continued, and I soon went on to realize how the silence around us was talking to us. Beyond the rustle of leaves, the distant call of birds, and the crunch of our footsteps on the gravel it was like the mountains had their own language, unmapped and wildly irrelevant.

Then there was the silence of the stranger. This wasn't an uncomfortable or awkward silence. The silence was one that made room to be fully present with my own thoughts and feelings.

It made me wonder: how often do we truly listen? To ourselves and the world around us – not just to others. How often do we just sit there in silence, and let it teach us?

It hit me like a breath of fresh air. Life had become chaotic, and I had so lost myself in the frenzy to fill the silence (to do, to achieve, to prove). I had forgotten the value of just being.

Reflection for the Reader

Have you ever felt like your own mind is drowning in noise? If you have ever longed for a moment of stillness and then it's uncomfortable or even unbearable, perhaps it isn't the stillness that is the issue.

If you haven't, you're not alone. For silence is intimidating… nothing but air to spare… and I see myself. It's also a gift; it's a space where we can hear what really matters.

The silence was my teacher as I walked through the mountains. I learned to let go of the wanting for answers, dance with the questions, and trust the process.

I invite you to do the same, then. Discover your present moment of silence, a moment to stop and listen, a moment to be. What you might find is surprising.

The Stillness Ahead

By the time we came to our next resting point, the sun was already on its way down and was starting to paint the fields of the mountain's orange and pink. The stranger merely motioned for me to come to sit with him, and without a word stared out toward the view.

After a long time, we sat there in silence and the beauty of the moment was hitting us. I heard something shift in that stillness, I felt a quiet peace, a quiet acceptance, that I was exactly where I was supposed to be.

We weren't even close to the end, but for the first time, I wasn't in a hurry to get to the end. I had learned from the mountains, that the lesson is in the path, and I was ready to hear.

> ## Reflection for the readers
>
> *Before moving forward with the lessons of stillness, I invite you to consider how your own relationship with quietness will guide you into deeper stillness. What does it reveal to you? What does it teach you?*
>
> *And sometimes the greatest wisdom isn't something we say, but rather something we're willing to hear.*

It seemed that in the mountains time compressed itself, all the hours flattening down into minutes, and what feels like lifetimes into days. As the trail continued, I started to learn how to accept the silence (perhaps not fully accept it, but I was learning to make peace with it). The quiet, however, was not quite empty. It was alive, alive with a rhythm I was only now just starting to catch the undertones of.

The Weight of Stillness

That morning, as we left, the man strode ahead, his march set but not hurried. My thoughts raced behind, I had yet to ask questions I had. I didn't understand so much of him or where we were heading, or what it was even I was searching for. But I held my tongue. I didn't want to break the spell, the spell of understanding that was forming between the two of us, the fragile sound of silence.

Its path, now, snaked through dense forest. It was cool in the air, heavy with pine and damp earth. The silence deepened and the world's noises softened, clutching us in its cocoon.

This wasn't the type of silence I had known: the pauses in conversation that felt uneven, the weighted moments broken up by the banality of the city. This silence was different. It wasn't nothing, and at the same time it was something; it was a presence as if the forest itself was listening, waiting for me to do the same.

It was almost unbearable to the weight. I wanted something to pull me away from the stillness, something that would poke at my thinking. My mind became a noisy passenger, throwing out thoughts like stones into the stillness: What's next? How much farther? What did I have to leave behind for this?

Then the stranger turned and spoke as if sensing my struggle. "Do you hear it?"

The long stretch of silence ended with his startled voice. "Hear what?" I asked. He gestured around us. "The silence. Do you hear it?"

I gave a frown, not knowing what he meant. You don't hear silence; it is a lack of sound. Or so I thought.

Then I was there, standing there, closing my eyes, and I felt it, the faint rustle of leaves, the slightest of distant chirps, the regular beat of my own breath. But the silence wasn't empty. It was full, brimming with life that I had not noticed I had been too distracted with.

"They didn't go mute, they weren't muffled…it's not the silence that's loud," he said, as though answering my own thought process. "It's your mind. Quiet that and you'll hear everything."

And they continued, and his words stayed with me. I couldn't stop thinking about it, that noise in my head, the constant chatter that had haunted me my entire life. I only knew it was taking up all that space then and drowning out everything else.

Have you ever sat in silence and your thoughts overfilled you? You try to tame a wild animal—fight it all you want, but it won't be tamed. That's what my mind felt like: Restless, untamed, not willing to surrender.

The mountains though had their way, whether you were ready or not. The more I walked, the heavier I felt my own inner chaos. I remembered what my life was like back in Mumbai— all the meetings, all the deadlines, all the channels buzzing with notifications. I had done so much during my days, yet I realized, finally, how empty they really were.

The silence made me see myself more clearly. It wasn't the version of me that people write down into titles or accomplishments; it was simply me at my rawest, unfiltered self. And that truth was messy. It was vulnerable. It was uncomfortable.

I wanted to run from it, to fill the silence with something, as long as it kept me distracted from myself. However, the stranger, always patient, noticed my discomfort.

One evening as we got to a clearing that could overlook the valley, he said "Sit." The day was coming down, as mountain peaks were painted in gold and amber.

I sat beside him, my legs folded beneath me. He didn't say anything, didn't explain. All he did was close his eyes, sit still, and control his breathing into a rhythm, slowly and steadily.

I tried to do what he was doing but my mind wouldn't comply. I started thinking about a bunch of things, one just as loud as the next. What am I doing here? How long do we have to sit? Is this even worth it?

Minutes felt like hours. The pain was starting in my legs, my back started to protest, and he didn't budge.

And then, something shifted. I started noticing my breath somewhere between my frustration and my surrender. The steady, unchanging way it would move in and out. It kept me grounded, even with my thoughts wanting to pull me away.

Not sure if it was enough or not, but it was enough to quiet the noise, at least for a moment.

Learning from the Mountains

As the Day passed and the silence ceased to be menacing and became something of a friend. The way the wind whispered through the trees, the way the sunlight danced on the river's surface, the way my body moved in time with all of that, things which I had never noticed before, things I had never paid attention to.

The stranger did not speak often, but when he did, they sounded like stones dropped into a still pond, then rippling out.

One morning he stopped to ask me, "Why the mountains seemed so still?"

What was he trying to say, I thought for a moment. "Because they don't move?" I offered.

He smiled. "Because they have nothing to prove… They simply are."

His words hit me deeply. I had spent how much of my life trying to prove something to somebody, to something, to anyone. I had wasted how much energy just chasing validation, when the mountains stood tall and proud, needing none of that?

It was a simple lesson, but profound. The mountains taught me what it meant to be present, to be in my own stillness, in their stillness, and in that there wasn't anything to be but my own body.

Reflection for the Reader

I can't help but wonder as I write this: how often do we allow the noise of our world to silence the silence inside of us? How often do we chase things that don't matter when we could be listening to stillness?

> *Silence is more than not listening to sound. It's a space, a mirror, and a teacher. It shows our fears, our worries, our hopes, and our truths.*
>
> *Therefore, I give you the invitation to take a moment of silence in your life. It's not just the silence of turning off your devices or finding a way to be quiet, it's the silence of sitting with yourself — your thoughts, your breath, your being.*
>
> *It won't be easy. It will be unbearable, at times. It is something that still speaks to you if you're willing to sit with it and hear it whisper to you.*

A Step Toward Stillness

All this fed into me while we got to the next resting point, and by that time I felt light, not physically, but emotionally and spiritually. The mountains hadn't changed, yet I had. At first, the silence was so heavy it suffocated me, now it was an old friend that I was only just starting to understand.

That stranger didn't talk much, but his presence said a lot. I saw in his silence the stillness I was teaching myself to practice.

But we weren't there yet; in fact, for the first time in in my life, I wasn't rushing to get to the destination. I was learning how to trust the path, and to be still, and let it teach me the lessons that only it can.

About an hour later the fire crackled and the stars began to poke holes in the dark of night and I felt a sense of something

I hadn't known in years. The silence wasn't empty. That box was packed, oh, how it was packed with life lessons and possibilities.

The rustic light had added an extra hum to the night, a distant rustle of leaves, an insect chirp now and again, and the lulling whispers of the river below. I had begun to accept the silence, but a small part of me remained equally desperate to know the answers, to gain clarity, to hear words as I once did.

The stranger across from me, always enigmatic, sat with his face lit from the flickering amber flames. He had said so little on our journey, but he said so much. He knew the questions in my heart before I could even string them into words.

"Why should silence be uncomfortable?" Breaking the stillness, I asked.

After a long moment, he looked at me and replied. "It's tough because it forces you to meet yourself."

A Mirror to the Soul

There was something about the mountains, about the silence that would deprive you of things, peel back the layers of pretense, and let the raw truth show. Until now, I considered silence as something vacant, and meaningless. But, here, it was. Alive. Pulsating with life lessons I had avoided for years.

Have you looked at your reflection for far too long? At first, it's all you see, the surface of your familiar face, expressions you've polished for years. The longer you stare, the more you realize you start to see what's underneath: the worn-out eyes, the fears that aren't said, the vulnerabilities you try so hard to disguise.

The silence felt like a mirror I couldn't turn away from. This was not just who I was, but who I had become, out of lack of stillness.

Days became nights and I started to pick up the patterns in what I was thinking. The fears repeated like a broken record, the doubts seeped in unnoticed at any provocation, the urge to control what I could not let myself be.

The stranger always watching offered me a bit of advice that changed me. When I first heard that, it intrigued me about it. "It only reveals. The judgment comes from you."

As the morning was waking up the peaks, he took me to a small clearing in which the river split itself into two streams, which then found their own path down through the rocks. He flicked his hand for me to sit and watch.

We sat there observing the water's dance, in silence for hours. It went as smoothly as a thing could, with complete disregard for obstacles. It just adjusted when it hit a rock, even if it was a rock being flattened; it didn't resist, it didn't stop, it carved a new path through the rock or it gently went around it.

Eventually, he asked, "What do you see?"

I hesitated. "The river's moving, it's adapting."

He nodded. "And what do you feel?"

Letting the sound of the water fill me, I closed my eyes. "I feel… at peace. That's the river: It doesn't fight; it just moves forward."

"That is its wisdom," he said. "To flow is to trust. To resist is to suffer."

His words hit me deeply, I couldn't even put into words how they resonated. How many times had I fought the current instead of the current of my own life and the illusion of control only to work myself into exhaustion?

That day the river taught me the beauty of surrender: instead of weakness, it was a source of strength.

The silence became a ritual the further along we traveled. Beds by the river or beneath the pines began each morning with an hour of stillness. For a second, I told my mind to shut off, as it fought against the stillness, throwing some distraction upon every other thought it could conjure up. Eventually, I figured out how to accept those thoughts, just like they accept to be carried away by the stream.

The stranger handed me a notebook and a pen one night. "Write," he said simply.

"What should I write?"

"What it tells you without sound."

It stared back at me like a blank page. And so, as I started to write those words poured out of me like a river, unfiltered, unpolished, but most certainly honest.

I put on paper my fears and my hopes, my regrets. I wrote about the man I was and the one I wanted to be. And in the process, I discovered something unexpected: **clarity**. I realized that silence was not emptiness. We were taking up space—space for truth, for true understanding, for true transformation.

Reflection for the Reader

Have you taken the time to listen to your own voice, quiet and to yourself? The kind of silence that is not achieved by switching off the outside noise, but by switching off and listening to whatever comes from inside?

It's not easy. Silence will challenge you, and confront you oftentimes into frustration. Except, it will also teach you—about yourself, about the world, and about the things that really do matter.

I invite you to pause and stop all that is moving in your own life. Even when it's uncomfortable, sit with it. Listen to what it has to say. You're going to be surprised when you see what you find. And when you find it, write it down.

A Shared Stillness

One day as we sat by the fireplace, I was sitting next to the stranger and I thought to myself, I will ask the stranger the question that has been bothering me. "So why is it we're so terrified of silence?"

He didn't answer right away. Instead, he continued poking the fire and watching the flames dance in the darkening sky, he finally said "Silence is the mirror of the soul, most people aren't ready to see it."

These words stuck in my head for a long time, after the fire downed. I contemplated how many times, throughout my life, I had tried to fill my life with noise: work, distractions, random conversations—that way I wouldn't have to sit with myself. In the mountains, there was nowhere to run from it. I was learning to embrace it slowly.

When we arrived at the stop of our trek, I had already changed. The silence was no longer so intimidating, it was an old friend now. It didn't wipe away all of my fears or doubts, but it did provide me with the room to do the work.

The stranger was, as always, observant; he noticed the change. Sat watching the stars one evening, he said to me, "You're beginning to understand."

I nodded [...] without knowing how to say. But he was right. I grasped, not just the silence, but myself.

They could teach you things a book or conversation never could. It was a teaching by experience, by being there, by the simple act of being. I didn't know I had strength until I found it in that silence.

I discovered that the silence had not ended. It was a gateway for the lessons yet to be learned. The stranger didn't explain anything, didn't promise anything; he just took me by the hand and led me, step by step, farther into the journey.

The mountains remained unchanged, but I saw them differently. They weren't landscapes – they were reflections, teachers, and companions on this path of self-discovery.

As we carried on, I was thankful for the silence, the ideas, the things I had learned, and for the trek in front of me. I still had the next part of the journey ahead but right now; I was happy to sit with the stillness and learn what words never could. Silence was slowly stripping away the layers of protection I had built around myself. And in that silence, I found the strength I never knew I had.

CHAPTER 5

ARRIVAL AT THE CAVES

The Last Ascent

Ahead wound and steep, barely visible in fading sunlight, was the path I hadn't envisioned. Every step was like negotiating with the terrain, the mountains felt like they were trying to prove something to me. Now the air was thinner, with a crispness that implied the altitude we had climbed. Towering peaks felt like emerging from the clouds and touching the sky.

I stole a glance at the stranger. He was walking steadily, unflinchingly; it was like he'd walked this path a thousand times before. By now I started trusting him without question—something about his movements was calm, but a part of me remained surrounded by mystery. I didn't even know his name. Following a person with a blank slate for an identity was strange and yet there I was tethered to him, following him further into the unknown.

It was a grueling climb and with every step my legs burned. Instead, it was the physical strain that didn't wow me—it was the silence. It wasn't silent in the way of an emptiness, or a void, but was a silence so full of life that I could almost hear the earth whispering. Occasional cracks of a branch underfoot, a distant

Arrival at the Caves

bird call or the rustle of leaves all seemed somehow magnified, as if the mountain itself spoke.

Then I realized how infrequently I'd actually let myself hear things. Silence had always been that—something to fill up with sound, distraction, or work—something absent, something to be moved beyond so you could get back to what really mattered. However, on this sacred path, the silence was a presence that must not be denied the right to attention, reflection, and surrender.

We climbed onto a narrow ridge, and my guide indicated we should stop. Pointing toward the skyline where the sun was setting, he made his gesture. For a moment, I forgot I was tired; I was looking at the sheer majesty of the view.

"It's beautiful," I murmured. A faint smile played at his lips, and he nodded but did not speak, and he didn't seem to want me to. Like he wanted me to sit with my thoughts rather than tell him anything. This ascent was the most challenging in its nature of the trek. Sheer drops flanked one side of the path; jagged rock faces the other. It was cold in the air now, and the wind blowing around us just made me feel both invigorated and humbled.

It wasn't long before doubt crept in, could I really do this? My guide stopped, and though I wouldn't have thought it possible, there he was looking at me. He didn't speak, but he spoke with his eyes. His eyes locked me in as if he was saying it silently in my ear, "You've got this." I took a deep breath and started to push forward one step at a time. It was as if each step was a statement of faith, in the path, and in myself.

The First Glimpse

I saw them when we rounded the last turn. The caves were not typical at a glance, they were hidden, hugging the mountainside. The entrances were no grand slabs. No elaborate carvings. There were only dark quiet openings that seemed to beckon with a mystery all of their own.

The closer we got, I could feel it; like some great energy oozing out of them — out of the caves themselves. I didn't know what it was, I couldn't see it, or pick it up with my hands, but I felt it in my chest — a resonance that rooted me deeply and lit me up simultaneously.

The entrance leads to a bigger cave. He said finally, his voice low and steady, "Wait here." He had not spoken for a long time. With no further word, he entered the cave, leaving me to my thoughts. I sat on a stone nearby as he gestured for me to do so. There I was, who overcame the stillness of the mountains, sitting there taking in the nature around me, and still in awe of what was about to unfold.

As I waited, the reality of where I was started to sink in. I had escaped the concept of familiarity, the safety of the city, and even the identity that I had given myself for so long. And now I stood here on the brink of something I didn't know how to explain.

Around me were the mountains, alive with being, comforting and awe-inspiring. There were whispers carried by the wind, but not words. Feelings – **strength, resilience, and surrender.**

Arrival at the Caves

I breathed the crisp mountain air, closed my eyes, and filled my lungs. I found I had a strange peace at that moment. I didn't know what I was going to do there but I knew I was exactly where I was supposed to be.

My guide reappeared, and he wasn't alone. Behind my guide, trailing, were six figures, their silhouettes against the dim light of the cave. I gasped when I saw them step into the open.

Of them three wore deep, earthy robes, there was a sense of steady vigor, their eyes calm, but intensely so. The other three, swathed in lighter tones, moved with a nurturing grace and fluid grounded in quiet wisdom. They seemed to together embody the perfect balance of earth and sky, strength and grace, opposites that seemed perfectly whole.

Looking at them, you could tell each one had quiet authority, their faces carried a look of peaceful wisdom like they possessed lifetimes of wisdom. Their silence was one of knowing, depth, and another feeling I couldn't put a label to; they hadn't spoken.

The monks nodded to the stranger and then turned to me. I looked up under their gaze and felt as if every layer I had so carefully built around myself had been laid bare. But instead of judgment, it was acceptance, an unconditional acceptance that was coming from someplace beyond words.

One of them stepped forward, moving deliberately and fluidly. Calmly and kindly, she looked and placed a small bowl of water before me. She gestured at me to drink, without a word. The act itself was so ordinary, but it was profound. Sipping the water from the bowl to my lips, it was cool, and it was refreshing, but it was more than that. I felt it grounding, as though it polished away the complexity I had lost in the haze of my old life.

In silence, the monks watched—in their steadiness and unwavering presence it felt as if they were holding space for something more than what the moment was. And that was all I knew, and in that stillness, I felt a flicker of understanding, a flicker of understanding which was the first step on a path I was only beginning to see.

A Sacred Welcome

The monks waved for me to follow them inside the cave, and I paused for a moment looking back at my guide. He didn't say anything but gave me a gentle nod. This instilled in me enough courage to do what needed to be done.

Inside, the cave was bigger than it looked on the outside; its walls were smooth and felt cool to the touch. No artificial light, it was just a flicker of a small fire in the center with its glow casting dancing shadows up the walls.

Their presence is commanding and yet, at the same time, balanced. Each had their own energy; some steady, some fluid, and some nurturing, yet each at the same time, grounded and elevated the space. A monk had arranged for me to sit in a grass aasan. One even laid down a bowl of fruit nearby. Already I knew that I was not being welcomed as a guest, but as a person who belonged.

Cross-legged, I sat on the aasan, the firelight warming my face. The monks surrounded the firelight, their movements fitting together as if as part of a bigger whole.

The silence deepened, and then. I recall a noiseless noise that did more than simply permeate into my pores... It permeated all of who I was. It wrapped around me, both comforting and conflictive.

I could almost touch the weight of walking the journey to this point in the silence—not the journey of the body, but the paths of the heart and of the soul.

I didn't know what would come next. As I sat there surrounded by these enigmatic figures, I started to feel anticipation in the sense that something big was going to happen. And so, I waited. I came here because of the mountains. The silence had prepared me.

A Name Revealed

My guide entered the circle, as the silence became more profound. But for the first time, the monks' attention shifted, their eyes touching on him, and with a reverence that couldn't be questioned. He lowered himself across from me onto the aasan, how he did so was deliberate and unhurried, like a man who stretched time out with casual ease.

Feeling his voice break the silence like the first drop of rain that had fallen after a long, long drought, he quietly spoke. "I think it's time." Me being me "Time for what?" I wanted to ask, but there was something in his presence that stopped me. It was not a time to talk—it was a time to listen.

He stared at me like he was looking into my questions and my doubt. His silence was always deep to the point it unnerved and intrigued me simultaneously. And yet, now, there was something different: A change, and behind it, the shifting senses from ready responding.

He began: "My name is **Rudra**." His voice was steady and clear.

The name lingered in the air, infused with as much meaning as one could pack into it, it bound around me like a cloak. 'Rudra.' The name wasn't just a name, it was an invocation. It sounded like it echoed off the walls of the cave, echoing in the surrounding space, in my chest too.

I stayed there staring at him, stunned; the weight of the moment hitting me: Rudra. In Sanskrit where the name means Shiva, the destroyer, the transformer — the one that makes space for new beginnings. It was not just the name, a symbol of strength, and power; it was symbolic of those immortal unions, the eternal dance of creation and dissolution.

I remembered there were a million times I had asked him his name on the trek and memories flashed through my mind in that instant. I had been insistent, inquisitive, and even annoyed at times. Every time I asked "Who are you?" or "What should I call you? " and sometimes "What is your name?" he only smiled—a quiet, knowing smile, gesturing toward the horizon. Many times, he responded cryptically, and said, "You'll know when the time is right." I had no idea when, and I was sure my curiosity would kill me.

I asked him again by the riverside as the river's sound roared around us. Nevertheless, his response had been the same — patient silence as though my question was not urgent with regard to the road that lay before.

As I saw him sitting before me now, I understood the truth. It wasn't secrecy or mystery he'd been withholding his name over. He'd been waiting. For me to get here, to be ready. Rudra. Then, the name of the man ran through my mind, its weight, its significance.

He went on, his voice introspective but firm. "It's not a name I chose. It's a name given to me by people. A name is not only an identity but it's also a walk of the path you walk."

I realized it was like a wave. But this man wasn't ordinary; this enigmatic guide who brought me through the mountains, endured my questions without answering them directly. It wasn't just a coincidence that he was there; his presence was almost fated, it was purposeful.

Hesitantly, breaking the silence, I asked "Why now?" My voice still felt small, subtotal, in the sacred room among us.

A small, knowing smile spread across his face—the faces of hundreds of lifetimes were compressed into that small smile. "Now you're ready to hear it," he said simply as if those were the answers I'd been searching for. And he was right. Now I understood the name, the man, the moment. I hadn't been ready before. I needed the trek, the challenges, the moments of self-doubt, and the silences, to take away my fundamentals and my diversions. I could understand now the gravity of who he was and why he showed up in my life?

Rudra. It wasn't just his name. But it was the key, the key to the lessons I still had to learn, the truths I still had to discover, the transformation, that was already occurring within me.

The Seven Monk's

Rudra invited me to follow him outside the cave, and we stepped out together. Above us, the night sky seemed to go on forever, the stars that filled this canopy letting out a soft, ethereal glow. The air was crisp, only slightly tinged with the faint whiff of pine and earth, affording me that grounding sensation that many call *'reality'* as my mind frantically tried to take everything in.

He brought me over to a gorge that overlooked the valley. Over the warmth of the earth, the dark silhouette of the Ganga wrapped itself like smoke among mountains. Rudra said, very softly, "I want you to see something."

I took his gaze towards the cave perched at the slope. I could see six figures in a circle around a faint glow of firelight, from this distance. Still, they gave off an inconceivable feeling of completeness, as if they already knew the secrets of the universe.

Rudra broke the silence. "Each of them has a fragment of wisdom," he said, respectfully. "They are those who guard the great energies, the guardians that have aligned with Ancient

Truths of existence. They symbolized balance, harmony, and spiritual evolution in one."

To the gravity of his words, I turned to him. "What kind of wisdom?" I said, faltering along, my voice barely audible behind the words.

His gaze softened and then Rudra began to explain, his voice was steady and methodical as though he had been born to explain the way in which rivers flow past stone.

Adira – Stability (Sthiratva) He pointed toward this first monk, who sat with a deportment as rooted as if she was one with the earth herself. "That is Adira," Rudra began. "She reminds us of the importance of being rooted. To be rooted is to create a kind of base that can withstand the storms of life. Without stability, even the strongest tree cannot grow." I watched Adira, and I knew Rudra was right. Stability was more than just standing firmly: it was being strong in one's roots, unshakeable in the midst of fierce winds.

Ishani – Compassion (Karuna) Rudra looked over at a monk whose presence cast such warmth and connectedness. He carried on. "That is Ishani," he said. "She teaches us the power of empathy and love. (The word) compassion is the bridge between mind and heart reminding us that strength lies not in domination, but connection." I think back to times when compassion has grown and felt like a lifeline. This wasn't only about being kind; this was about seeing ourselves in others and working from that shared humanity.

Kapeesh - Discernment (Viveka) Rudra dipped his head at the figure whose gaze could pierce through anything; he could, as if, see the very fabric of truth. "That Kapeesh," Rudra said, pointing to the next monk. "He is one who possesses the wisdom to perceive without the eyes, to listen without the ears, to go where no one has ever been, to gather brothers and sisters of different races and nations into one family and enable human hearts everywhere to probe the deepest mysteries of being and the true meaning of life. The ability to trust your intuition and perceive what's not there is called discernment." Too many times, have I tried to ignore my instincts, only to actually realize how much they were trying to steer me. Clarity wasn't the only thing that discernment entailed; it was also courage derived from inner vision.

Sarthak – Courage (Sahas) Rudra pointed at a monk who exudes quiet strength, "That is Sarthak," he said. "He symbolizes courage, that fire inside of us. It is the energy to act even in the face of fear. There is no such thing as fearlessness, it's just about moving forward regardless." A rush of heat filled me, as Rudra spoke. Courage was something I've heard my whole life, but courage didn't mean some ideal; it meant acting despite uncertainty. It was bravery for what I had done on such a great journey.

Varya – Introspection (Antarmukha) Pointing to the next monk, Rudra said "That is Varya. She teaches the art of what to do inside of our heads. The art of going inward. What does it feel like when we don't know what to do with our heads? She teaches self-reflection; how to get clear in the stillness of our being. Helps

Arrival at the Caves

to see, introspect, allowing us to navigate into the depths of our emotions and get to the true truth." I closed my eyes for a moment and felt the weight of wisdom here. How often had I not faced inward, lost in the din of the world? It was a reminder that the answers I wanted, were inside me all the time.

Vyom – Creation (Srishti) Rudra pointed out towards the last monk in the circle whose energy seemed to be through the roof. "That is Vyom," he said. "He teaches us the power of manifestation, the ability to transform thoughts into reality. Creation is not merely about producing—it is about aligning intention with expression, bringing dreams to life." The words rippled through me; I knew their truth. Creation is more than action, but a sacred act of co-creation with the universe, a reminder of our limitless potential.

My whisper, as I turned to Rudra. "And you?" His eyes were deep, I couldn't understand them yet, he met my gaze. He just said, "I am the **seventh, surrender. The ultimate wisdom**: to let go, I teach to trust the flow of life, and liberation through acceptance. Surrender is not giving up ... it is about aligning with the infinite rhythm of existence." He said, and his words fell over me like a spell, but it was deep and unshakeable. Surrender was the wisdom of the universe I had found most difficult to surrender to; the one I was most afraid of. None of it seemed truer than this right now.

His words weighed as heavy as the mountains in the vast silence of the heavy air. The names, the fragments of wisdom – each had an echo that stirred deep within me. This wasn't just a lesson, but an initiation to a better knowing of itself and of the universe.

Suddenly Rudra put a hand on my shoulder and said as if he could hear my thoughts: "You are not here by chance. You've always had the fragments of wisdom inside of you. The monks are not separate from you … they are mirrors, they are noticing what you're already carrying."

The monks would have shimmered in silhouettes, eternal silhouettes that ground in their presence. Each was a facet of the infinite, and in combination, they made a circle, balanced, whole energies.

I was certain, at that moment, that I was not at the end of the journey. It was only the beginning. Those fragments of wisdom would lead me, but I had to awaken them within me. I was ready for the first time.

Completing the Circle

On our way back to the cave, my eyes saw it differently. Its embers glowed softly from the fire at its center, which had all but gone out. The circle of monks sat serene, yet powerfully so. The last one stepped into the circle, making his way to stand among them, completing the circle's formation, humming with an almost palpable energy made up of strength and grace, grounding and inspiring. I paused briefly, I didn't know where I fit. One of the monks gestured for me to sit, motioning deliberately.

I sat myself down on the aasan, and I could feel myself belonging. This was no damn formation, it was an invitation to be part of a circle that didn't just exist anymore, but rather was an invitation to be part of something timeless, something sacred.

Surrounded by the seven monks and in that silence, it's the fragments of that wisdom that came alive. They weren't just lessons to learn, but energies to be activated — stability, compassion, discernment, courage, introspection, creation, and surrender.

For the first time, I understood: The reason that this journey wasn't about finding something outside of me. Uncovering what had really been there was what it was about. The monks were mirrors, as was the cave, as was Rudra, reflecting the potential inside of me.

The silence grew heavier and I closed my eyes, allowing myself to accept the wisdom fragments and the continuing pilgrimage.

The Power of Stillness

In the hours that followed I was in a blur of stillness and reflection. The monks didn't speak, but I knew they were speaking with me on a level that had nothing to do with words. They were a mirror, reflecting back on my parts that had been buried and ignored.

Then I realized silence wasn't only an absence, but was a teacher, a language everyone could speak without words, a language which flowed freely amongst these monks, and it was natural — they were both steadfastly stable and deeply nurturing. It pushed me to face the fossil fuel of my own head — the thrum and rumble of fear and doubt preventing me from the inevitable.

Silence was working its magic and I started seeing glimpses of clarity. I did not see the pain I had carried so far was a burden but the lesson. I saw fear I had been running from, and that was not as an enemy, but as a guide.

The fire burned lower into the night and became little more than glowing embers. The space was grounded as the monks remained seated.

Breaking the silence Rudra said, his voice soft, but firm. "It's not an easy journey you've started. It will require more of you than you believe that you need to offer. It will give you more than you ever thought possible."

His words sat heavy in the air, reverberating through me as much as himself.

I didn't know what lay ahead. I didn't know that the monks would teach me any lessons, or what truths I would find. But I knew this: I was meant to be where I was.

That cool stone of the cave underneath me was peaceful, I hadn't felt that in years as I lay down that night. It was like the mountains helped me carry the weight I had for so long.

I didn't know all the answers, in fact, none of them. But, for the first time, I was alright with it. Sometimes the answer doesn't come in words – it comes with silence.

The Depth of Surrender

In the cave, among the quiet wisdom of the monks (each adding an individual essence), Rudra's gravity increased. He was more than just a guide who had steered me through the mountains in silence. When he revealed to me, he was one of the seven monks, an understanding of him, and an understanding of me, shifted profoundly.

"Most people don't understand what surrender actually means," Rudra's voice one evening, slow and quiet. The dancing of his words matched the dancing shadows that the firelight cast across his face.

"It's not giving up," he added, focusing on me. "It's not resignation or passivity. To surrender, it's to let go of what you think you know, what you think you need, but rather stepping into the unknown with faith."

His words rang true to me. How many times had I clutched at control, certainty, the fantasy that controlling every situation was even an option? How many times had I not done something out of fear of change, not because of a principle?

Rudra looked intently toward me and leaned forward. "Control is an illusion. The tighter that thing binds you, the more you cling to it. Freedom, true freedom, comes from surrender, from surrender not to the external forces, but to what is the essence of life right now."

He was speaking and that reminded me of that river we'd crossed on our trek. The current on Ganga was powerful and unforgiving, its waters had cut paths through the trees themselves over the centuries. Such a force would be futile to combat. To trust its flow was power, however—due to its flow to move with it.

Rudra said as if he had read his thoughts: "Surrender is not weakness. It's the courage to disembark from what doesn't benefit you anymore. It is the strength to trust in the process although the end is unknown."

The moments I had been forced to surrender on this journey came to mind, as I had felt as if it could not be overcome, only depending on Rudra's silent path. It had been the letting go of what was, one step at a time, faith that it would all be okay, despite not knowing what lay ahead.

Here I was sitting and I realized that surrender wasn't just a lesson. It was a way of being.

The River as a Metaphor

The river was ever present in our journey and Rudra's teachings often returned to it. One evening, his voice was the same rhythm as the river flowing. "It carves its way through obstacles as it moves, with patience and persistence. It isn't afraid of what it doesn't know—it knows that every curve of the road is a part of its trip."

I watched the current as it flowed steadily through the valley, and stood, beside the Ganga. It moved with a quiet power, an unspoken lesson in its constancy. The river wasn't just moving forward, the river was evolving, it was adapting, it was swimming over everything with no resistance, changing the land over time.

He continued: "Life is like the river. Slowly, but surely, one can feel it drifting away. But when we trust and have faith in the river, it will take you where you need to go, but only if you

Arrival at the Caves

stop … trying to control the course. The more you resist it, the more hassle you'll have. But when you let go you will discover a strength that is greater than you've ever known."

The faint roar of water carried his words into the cool night air. The Ganga, its twists and turns, seemed to represent me or at least my path, chaotic and beautiful at the same time.

I was still taking in Rudra's teachings, and his dual role as guide and monk both appeared in my head at the same time. He was the man who had walked beside me ever since, uncomplainingly taking my doubts and questions into his physical being, as he sat amongst the monks with all the wisdom and calm.

"Why didn't you let me know who you were?" On an evening that I could no longer keep the question bottled up inside. Rudra smiled faintly. "Would it have mattered?"

I frowned and didn't know quite how to respond. Silently, but without judgment, he said, "You weren't ready. "You would've changed nothing if I had told you at the start. But what I know is that they needed to experience the journey themselves, the climb through the challenges, doubts, and surrender. Only then you could understand who I was and why I was there." he added.

His words made me pause. He was right. If he had revealed his identity earlier, I would have leaned on him like a crutch instead of learning from him. He didn't say a word, and he let me walk this path on my own terms, and find out how strong I truly was.

And sometimes the best gift a teacher can give is to let the student struggle, Rudra went on. "Struggle brings clarity. It shows what you're really made of."

But what I saw and felt, too, was the moments I doubted myself: when the trek was too much, when the silence of the monks was too much when surrender felt impossible. Rudra was there in each of those moments, not to answer but to allow me that space to answer myself.

The realization hit me at last and I said: "You've been both guide and teacher."

Rudra nodded, "It's the merging of Surrender and the journey within."

Surrender was not just an abstract theory with Rudra, surrender was practical tools and lessons to be applied at every stage of the journey.

One evening he had said, "Surrender is no single act. It's practice. You don't only give up once. You give up, over and over and over again, moment by moment, decision by decision."

And he urged me to look at my life and uncover what I was still clutching too tightly like—expectations, fears, or identities that no longer worked for me.

He asked, "What if you released your need to control? … Would you trust that what was to come would come as it should?"

I couldn't help but wonder, why did this matter so much? Why? And to surrender wasn't releasing, it was trusting. I realized that trust was the basis of every meaningful journey.

Arrival at the Caves

As I sat among the monks, I became more aware of their balanced energies. Three were steadfast, grounded, and firm, and the others were nurturing grace, fluid, intuitive, a perfect harmony that Rudra had described. In that moment it was not only about feeling their energies or lessons to learn, but energies to embody.

Rudra's role as the keeper of surrender was to tie it all together. What his teachings meant was letting go, but they were also about integrating the parts of our knowledge of life into a whole.

"The monks are not here to answer you," Rudra said. "They are here to show you the questions. Cherag, the answers are already within you."

As I reflected on his words, I felt a shift within myself. The journey wasn't about reaching a destination or achieving a goal. It was about transformation—about becoming the kind of person who could embody the wisdom of the monks and carry it back into the world.

The night grew deeper, the fire burning lower but the embers of its fire softly pulsating like a heartbeat. And yet there was stillness, as my breath began to rhythmically sound, a reminder to bring me back to the present.

Rudra stood as steady as ever. His voice was low but firm "It's about practice. ... it's important, every breath, every step, every moment to trust, not just the monks, but yourself."

His words cast down over me like a warm blanket to reduce the complexity of the present. I realized it was the act of giving in to the breath, the flow, and the rhythm of life itself, that adds up to surrender.

That night as I lay down on the cold stones of the cave the beat of my breath wasn't done with me yet. Inhale, exhale — It was as steady as a funnel of the river I had seen. The weight in each Inhale was of control, expectation, and fear, and with each exhale I could feel the grip starting to loosen, start to expel. The mountains were silent and steadfast; it felt like they carried the weight of all the thoughts, my worries, my fears which I no longer needed.

What came over me was a peace, not the only temporary peace that is felt when you step away from distraction, but rather a deeper peace, a peace that comes with connection. I realized that surrender wasn't the end of the journey. It was just the beginning.

CHAPTER 6

BREATH AS THE BRIDGE

The firelight flashed softly, the long cave shadows dancing. The embers crackled rhythmically, their slow, steady, crackle, helped to steady my heartbeat, but full of anticipation. The inside of the cave was cool and crisp and surprisingly calming. With it grew the faint scent of earth and wood smoke, grounding me in the present moment, as Rudra and the monks fell back into their stoic meditation stillness.

I stayed in that silence that followed feeling a shift in me like I was ready, maybe, for the next part of this transformative journey. It wasn't spoken, but I sensed it: Now was the time to delve deeper, to link the teachings offered by the monks with the very essence of life.

The Breath: A Portal

"Breath," Rudra said, his voice interrupting the silence, "is the bridge between the physical and the spiritual world, between the conscious and unconscious."

I had never thought of breathing like that. To me, breath had always been automatic and unremarkable, just a background process that would keep me alive, without ever really asking for my attention to it. Rudra's words rewrote it all.

"Our life cannot exist without breath," he continued, staring hard into the flickering fire. "But still, most people are clueless as to its power. Unconsciously they breathe shallowly, they remain disconnected from their bodies, their minds, and their spirits."

Seated to Rudra's left, Adria spoke for the first time. Her voice was calm but also carrying an impressive strength. "Inhale deeply and feel your feet on the ground. That's stability—anchored by your breath to what is happening right here right now, regardless of the winds of life attempting to uproot you," she said. "It roots you in the present, providing the foundation for balance and clarity. Just as the mountains stand firm against the winds, your breath anchors you in the middle of the chaos of life."

I felt a pang of recognition. How many times had I wasted hours, my mind tearing through a series of thoughts one after another, never considering just stopping and breathing?

Rudra continued, "Breath is not just a physiological function; it is **prana**—the life force, which flows through all living beings. It's the energy that infuses you, brings you together, and keeps you alive. When you're able to lean into it, its true potential it can become a tool for healing, transformation, and transcendence."

The word prana really hit me. A term I had heard countless times before but hadn't really understood. It was there at that moment I realized it wasn't just a concept; it was a lived experience just waiting to be brought out.

Process of Conscious Breathing

Rudra motioned for me to sit comfortably and, "Let us begin." In their circle, the monks sat, a sense of serenity and ground permeating their presence. Rudra instructed me to close my eyes and concentrate on my breath, to notice what I was breathing, and not to change it.

His voice was calm, as he directed "Inhale deeply, feel the air entering through your nostrils, down your throat and in your lungs. Hold it for a moment. Then slowly exhale, along with the air letting everything go that doesn't serve you."

It was strange at first the amount of attention I was paying to a normal action to breathe in, slowly fill up my lungs, and then let go of the air. But, as I followed his instructions I realized, that the longer I went, staying connected with my breath the more I could notice the subtleness, the cool cold air as it entered, the warm heavy air as I exhaled, the gentle up and down of my chest.

"Place one hand on your belly and the other on your chest," Rudra said, "now inhale so your belly extends with each inhale and contracts with each exhale. This is diaphragmatic breathing; breathing that brings your whole being into play."

As I changed my breath to a more conscious, deeper, more intentional breathing something really interesting happened. The tension in my shoulders began to melt. The noise in my mind started to settle. I found myself at ease. It felt as if I had opened a faucet connected to a well of warm, inner calm that had been there all along and was within reach.

Breath as a Mirror

"Your breath is a reflection of your state of being," Rudra said. "It becomes shallow and rapid when you're anxious. It slows and deepens when you are calm. You can understand yourself by observing your breath. And you can control your breath to change your state of being."

Ishani nodded softly, radiating her warm presence as she said. "We take in a breath and that's where our compassion starts. Our breath is a bridge that helps us to connect with ourselves and with others. In moments of silence, breath acts as your anchor to solace, and bridge to others."

As she said, I remembered times in my life when stress consumed me —My breath was unsteady, my chest was heavy, and my thoughts disarrayed. However, the stillness of the cave was the exact opposite of what I had experienced. My body relaxed, my breath steady, and all my thoughts clear.

Rudra continued, "It is the simplest tool and perhaps the most powerful. The present moment is available to you through your breath. It helps you quiet the mind, heal the body, and awaken the spirit."

As I opened my eyes to look at the monks. Their postures were effortless. Their faces were serene. You could easily tell that they have this art that it's not just some practice but their way of life.

The Prana-Shakti Connection

"It's the breath that carries prana," Rudra explained, "and prana is shakti, the divine energy that flows through all creations. Blockage in prana occurs just when your breath is shallow or irregular. But when your breath flows freely so does your prana."

Sarthak leaned forward, his posture radiating strength. He said; "While facing fear or uncertainty your breath is your ally. Trust it: Each deep inhale fills you with the energy to act, and each exhale unfolds the path ahead. Your breath will not fail you."

After I began following the practices that Rudra and other monks shared, I could feel the energy inside me as if it was a warm current flowing through me. It wasn't just physical but also emotional. Sarthak's words never left me, for courage was not attempting to block fears or doubt, but it was about making the decision to move forward anyway.

Pranayam is an ancient practice of breath control. It wasn't merely breathing; it was about controlling the flow of prana inside the body, balancing its energy, and utilizing it for the process of transformation.

He guided me through a very simple practice and said "Follow me. Close your right nostril using your thumb and inhale deeply through your left nostril. Now also close your left nostril using your ring finger and hold your breath for a couple of moments. Next, let go of the hold on the right nostril and exhale. Once all the air is out, breathe in this time through your right nostril where your left nostril is still blocked by your ring finger. Block your right nostril using the thumb and after a couple of moments let go of the hold on your left nostril to exhale. Alternate nostril breath is called Nadi Shodhana. It harmonizes your body and mind by balancing your energy channels."

I did as he instructed and there was an immediate shift. As I continued to focus on my breath and pull my attention away from the chatter in my mind. With each cycle, I could feel more centered, more aligned and more in the present.

The Breath of Life

"We are all connected by means of breath," Rudra said. "It is the bridge between the physical and the spiritual world, the conscious and the unconscious, the finite and the infinite." His words were simple yet carried the deepest truth. Breathing was more than just a biological function; it was a sacred link to a greater something. Its flow is always constant and unyielding, it reminded me of the Ganga which flowed through mountains and valleys, connecting everything it touched.

Rudra said, as though he could hear the thoughts in my head, "The Ganga flows through these mountains. And likely so your breath flows through you. Both of them are rivers of life: carrying energy, wisdom, and transformation."

I inhaled deeply, closed my eyes again, and imagined the breath as a river flowing through me. With each exhale, I wasn't holding on as much; I wasn't tensing; I wasn't feeling doubt; I wasn't trying to control the situation. At that moment I realized that the breath wasn't just a means of staying alive. Breathe is a teacher, a guide, a bridge — to the deepest parts of myself.

With every breath, the stillness of the cave deepened. My inhales and exhales felt like threads, that slowly but surely, spun me closer to something I didn't know I aimed for. Rudra's ever-so-attentive voice, deliberate, loud, and firm, encouraged me to go further. "Breath, and breath only, it is the only involuntary action you can consciously control," he said. "It's the anchor that helps you to pull yourself out of chaos into the present moment'."

But I thought about how I had breathed so often and for what? In the other world, I had left, breath was just a background rhythm, undercurrent and unnoticed. In this space, it was everything: a lifeline, a guide, a revelation.

Rudra made a motion for me to open my eyes. The fire had almost burned out and the shadows in the cave had become fuzzy embers. The space was grounded by the monks who sat quietly, still in silence.

I wanted to absorb all the knowledge and soak in the energy. But Rudra could see I was learning to absorb the energy of stillness and silence and said "Let us go deeper." He moved his body slightly as if his body and breath were in perfect alignment. "Close your eyes, now bring your awareness to the space between your breaths."

It was disorienting, at first. I knew the inhale, and I knew the exhale, but the pause, the brief moment of stillness between them was always missing. My mind raced ahead of the rhythm as I struggled to catch it.

I could feel my restlessness and so did Rudra, he said, "Do not chase it. Let it come to you. For an act of breathing isn't only a physical act, it is a prayer, a meditation, a sacred exercise, an act of existence. Conscious breath brings you into alignment with the divine."

Varya spoke, her words deep as the cave. "Introspection starts with the breath. You will find space for yourself in the quiet between your inhales and exhales. Fear not this meeting; for it is the meeting of the truth." I softened my concentration and focused on breathing again.

Eventually, I started to notice the pause between the inhale and exhale, the smallest sliver of stillness; where everything appeared to have come to a momentary standstill. It felt like I was empty of thought, lost my sense of time, and had entered a dimension, a space of pure potential. I was weightless in that space, floating in the flow of the unknown itself.

Rudra said, "This is yours to carry. This is your anchor, your bridge, your path." further explaining "This space is the starting point of transformation. It's the void where the old is dissolved and the new is born. A journey within, into the infinite is available to you when you master the awareness of this space."

Breath as a Healer

Next Rudra guided me through another practice, he mentioned it's called Bhastrika —the Breath of Fire. I had heard about this particular pranayam before but never understood its true potential. "It is the breath of vitality," he said. "It stokes the inner flame, purifies the body, and awakens the spirit."

First, he showed, breaths sharp and forceful, his abdomen swelling with every inhale, and his abdomen sucked in with every breath out. Then it was my turn.

"Sit upright. Put your hands on your knees," he instructed. "Inhale slowly, and then exhale really strongly through your nose. Allow your breath to move like the bellows of a fire."

First, the practice started startling me. As I settled into the rhythm of its short breaths and rapid bursts, my body began to feel warm. With every breath, the body heat increased and felt clearing all the chatter away and creating a clarity of thought.

"Let this breath be a purifier," said Rudra. "It burns away toxins in your body... your mind... your spirit. It allows the prana to flow freely." I could sense the energy rushing through me, vibrant and alive. It felt as if I had connected with synergy from life, which always existed, just hiding under the layers of stress and disconnection.

Letting Go

As the session continued, Rudra introduced another practice: Or, it is **Kumbhaka**, retention of breath. "When you pause between breaths, that is a sacred space, that is a moment in which nothing is expected of you. It's not a question of depriving yourself or simply holding your breath," he said, "it's in that stillness trust starts to grow. It is about creation. You make room for change in the stillness of retention, you create space for transformation."

He told me to take in a deep breath, hold it to the count of 4, and release slowly. Initially, it was a horrible clash between my instincts and my will, something I had never felt before. The more I practiced the more I realized its purpose.

"Surrendering is what kumbhaka teaches," Rudra said. "The pause is where you learn to trust. Believe the next breath is coming. Faith that you are held by something greater than yourself."

His words resonated deeply. How many times had I relied on control, not willing to release it? Simple yet profound practice that required me to release my grip on things and learn to let go, trusting the flow of life itself.

"Breath is not just a tool for the body," Rudra went on. "It is a bridge to the spirit. When you align your breath with intention, you connect with the divine energy that flows through all things."

Pranayama he spoke of not as physical exercise but as a meditation, a spiritual practice, a way to get into the rhythm of the universe. He said, "When your breath flows in harmony, so does your life. When your breath is chaotic, it represents your inner chaos."

The monks through their silence seemed to express this truth. They literally embodied a sense of balance — as if their breath was always in line with their being. Watching them I understood that this was all they practiced, and it was not necessarily about perfectness but harmony.

Rudra said the breath was like a river, flowing through the body constantly. "The Ganga flows through the mountains, carving its path and nurturing the ground, your breath flows through you, to nurture and shape you."

The analogy struck a chord. The thought came to me of the Ganga and its endless flow, the power it possessed to cleanse and renew. I realized my breath held the same potential. A force of transformation, a guide in the midst of this journey known as life. "Now, breathe with the same awareness," Rudra said, referencing the similar awareness of this river. "Let it take you, let it cleanse you, let it couple you with the greater whole."

Rudra ended the session by talking about how these practices must be integrated into daily life. "You are always with your breath," he said. "It's Your anchor, refuge, and guide. Use it to navigate the storms. Use it to find calm amongst the chaos. Use it to reconnect with the true essence of life."

He taught me what it means by conscious breathing, something I should do throughout the day, not only in stillness. "When you walk, breathe. When you work, breathe. Breathe when you go through challenges. The breath is to be your constant companion." I understood he meant to be aware of every breath not only during meditation but rather through every movement.

That night while I lay on the cool stone floor of the cave, I felt Rudra's words settle over me. What he'd taught me was more than techniques, they were the keys to a better understanding of myself and the world around me. I closed my eyes and took a deep breath, allowing my breath to pull me towards a state of calm. In the stillness I was grounded in a way I cannot explain; connected to something greater and greater than myself — the monks, the mountains, and the river.

I had never really realized the power of breath, until that moment. Just like that, sleep took me and I knew this was the beginning. The breath, as river Ganga was my companion through this journey within. And all it was one inhale and exhale at a time.

Breath as Connection

The rhythm of the cave's hush, the breathwork, Rudra's voice, and the still presence of the monks all collaborated together to turn the breath from a mere biological function to a portal of far more importance.

The breath, he described, connects not only us to ourselves but also to the world around us. "Every breath you take is a gift of the trees, of the oceans, of the mountains," he said. "And what you exhale every time is a gift, you return."

Vyom adds, in his vibrant, lively presence. "Breath is creation. It is the first act of existence, the force that brings life into being. With each breath, you participate in the ongoing act of creation. In a way what you inhale nourishes you, and what you exhale shapes the world."

His words are simple yet so powerful. "Breathing is a kind of dance, there is no losing, only giving and receiving from the universe. The Ganga keeps flowing, keeping everything on her path alive."

"Inhale with gratitude," Rudra advised. "Exhale with grace. This is how you praise the life force that sustains you."

Later on, during the session, I observed that the monks' presence magnified the teachings. Even as they made no sound, their breaths, slow, steady, rhythmic, became audible. In other words, their very being was in rhythm with the very natural rhythm of the universe.

Rudra gestured toward them. He said, "Watch their breaths. They are not separate from the mountain or the river or the sky. They are one with everything, everyone around and themselves."

I tried to imitate their rhythm, synchronizing my breath with their faint sound. As I did this, I felt a feeling of absolute unity, not only with the monks but with everything around us the entire space we were in. For me, I found that it reminded me that I was not alone, that my breath made part of a much bigger whole.

As I sat there, the flickering firelight framed in them, I realized that this journey was not about the mountains or the monks. It was about coming back to me, one breath at a time.

Reflection for the Reader

Hopefully as you have wandered with me through the lessons of Rudra and the monks, you have begun to feel the might of your own breath. Okay, so let's take a moment—try to bring a nice breath in through your nose, hold it there gently, and exhale it slowly out through your mouth. Feel that? It's life itself passing through you.

Now, ask yourself: When was the last time you acknowledged your breath deeply and honestly? Just not in a rushed, stressful moment of stress, or exhaustion, but with presence, with intention, with gratitude?

The breath is the one constant we have in our lives — we kiss it when it comes in and kiss it back as it leaves. And yet we take it for granted so often not realizing how this force of nature can guide, heal, and transform us.

Take another deep breath. Pay attention to how it feels this time. Is it shallow or deep? Calm or erratic? Think about what that says about you now, in terms of mind and body.

Here's a question to ponder: If you start to breathe consciously, what might change in your life? What if you approached each one, inhale as a gift and each exhale as what you construct in this world? What could this simple act of awareness mean for how you deal with stress, bring different people together, or manage life's challenges?

Try this:

In moments of stress: Take five deep, deliberate breaths — letting your exhale be longer than your inhale. Pay attention as your body starts to soften, and your thoughts start to settle.

In moments of joy: Draw a deep breath and then close your eyes, feeling happiness wash over you. Allow that moment to be magnified by your breath. And as you exhale give your gratitude.

In moments of reflection: Use your breath as a guide. As you breathe in, bring in clarity. Release distractions with each exhale.

As you go about your day, remember: Your breath is your anchor. It is always consistent, a constant bridge between your inner world, and the chaos of the outside world.

I was taught by the monks that the breath is more than just a physiological function, it's a sacred act of connection. Conscious breathing aligns you with life itself.

So, I leave you with this challenge: Take moments to simply breathe in the coming days. The only agenda or expectation is to breathe. Allow it to ground yourself, help you guide yourself, and that we are always given the infinite power to start again with each breath.

As you take the first conscious breath, remember this: You are not just breathing. You are healing, experiencing the deepest truth of living as you breathe in and you are constructing this world with every exhale.

CHAPTER 7

THE SACRED MUNDANE

Filling the Bucket

I had become accustomed to morning's silence, the silence that had become my companion, and I stepped into the fresh cold air outside of the cave. The monks were already awake, they moved slowly, and their presence grounding. Last night's fire had shrunk to glowing embers and some faint wisps of rising smoke.

They would take their sleek, soft blackness and fade into the background slowly and so completely that I had forgotten they were there, forgotten the speed at which I had spent my life, the rush in which the world had continued to reveal itself. But today felt different. The mountains themselves were holding their stillness for something to emerge, there was a subtle shift, a pause between breaths.

Approaching me deliberately, his gaze steady, as always, was Rudra. He handed me a wooden bucket, without a word. In front of the cave entrance, Adira, spoke, her voice low and controlled, centering me. "It's grounding every step," she said. "Let the task fix your mind as the mountains fix their mind to the winds."

The worn handle cracked slightly in my grip, bearing the marks of years of use, as they say. Rudra said nothing, simply, 'Today, you will fetch water.'

This wasn't a request and it wasn't a command. An invitation, a task put forth without a shred of understanding, much like the rest of it.

I took a look at the monks who were meditating near the fire. None of them looked at me, but their presence, their quiet support, was palpable and I imagined that they understood exactly what was about to happen.

"Where do I go?" I asked.

Rudra pointed towards the slope that ran down from the cave. "The stream," he said. "You'll find it."

He had spoken so simply, yet his words carried with them a weight about which I wanted to pause. I nodded and then started walking, the bucket swinging lightly at my side.

The Stream

With a narrow pine tree thicket from which the path wound down to the stream, the way to the stream was path was narrow. The air tonight was cool and fresh, and just faintly scented with moss and earth. With each step, I heard crunches of my boots on uneven ground.

I stopped at the stream when I got there and took it in. The crystal-clear water went smoothly splashing over smooth stones in a gentle cascade. Its sound was mellow, its melody a harmony with the mountains' silence.

The bucket dug into the stream and I knelt at the edge. It filled almost instantly with cold water rushing in. The bucket rose, and water slopped over its sides, wetting my hands and the earth at my feet.

The full bucket was heavier than I expected, pulling at the weight of my arm as I started to climb back to the cave. Descending hadn't seemed so bad, but now I felt the path was steeper and more difficult to climb. The handle pinched my palm, along with my pace catching up with me, and I slowed down, focusing on not spilling too much of the precious water.

My arm was trembling by the time I got to the cave and I could feel the pressure on my shoulder. I set the bucket down close by the fire, gasping for breath.

Rudra appeared again, calm, but observant. He gestured back towards the path, 'Again,' he said.

I blinked, confused. "Again?"

He nodded. "It has to be filled again several times." That is only the beginning of the water you have brought."

I wanted to protest, wanted to ask why this was even needed, but some power in his stare stared me down. His tone had no impatience, no expectation. All he was doing was presenting the task the way it was and letting me figure out how to work it out.

I sighed resignedly, grabbed the bucket and started descending again.

The Repetition

The first trip was much easier than the second. I was tired, my body tired and the bucket heavier with every step. The third trip was when my muscles started screaming in protest and the path seemed to go on forever.

The farther I climbed, the more my mind started to resist. Why am I doing this? What's the point? In fact, there is an easier way. Ishani's presence seemed to linger nearby, her earlier words echoing in my mind: "The first step of compassion is about you. The water is not about each trip," she said. "It's about the patience you pour into it."

It was an absurdly simple thing to do, almost maddening. Repeatedly when I got to the stream, I had to watch the water run over the edges of the bucket, erasing some of my efforts. I felt my body strain each time I climbed back to the cave.

But the repetition continued and started to change.

The frustration came first: this slow, creeping awareness at first. The water sparkled in the sun and I watched as it filled the bucket and noticed just how cool it was. As I climbed the slope, I noticed that my footsteps had a rhythm, the steady in–and–out of my breath.

What had been so mundane a few moments ago now started to have a different kind of texture. Fetching water wasn't just about fetching the water; it was about living that moment, about finding purpose in the purposelessness of getting the water.

A Quiet Revelation

For the fifth time as I knelt down by the stream, I stopped for just a bit longer than I had every other time. The water flowed over the stones and its surface caught the light in a way that struck me as almost magical.

But it hit me, the water didn't care about the stones in its way. It trickled around them and over them, without force, without struggle. Adira's earlier words returned to me: "Let the task root you."

It was then that I realized that I had been viewing the task with resistance, weakness, as an obstacle, instead of as an opportunity. The water, in its quiet wisdom, was teaching me something profound: to let go of my need to control and my expectations of the task and just be with what was.

Though the weight did not seem oppressive now, I carried the bucket back to the cave. But my mind still lightened the climb didn't seem so bad.

By the time I made it to the cave, Rudra was there, but his face was as unreadable as ever. Setting the bucket down and meeting his gaze, I felt good, good beyond the physical act.

He asked calm but probing, 'What did you learn?'

I had no idea what to say, so I stalled. I finally put in, "I learned... to let go." "To stop fighting just sit with the task."

Rudra nodded faintly smiling. The water's not the task, he said. It comes down to how you do it. There are lots of buckets to fill in life, some full and some empty. The question is, can you take them off with grace?"

I could hear him, but I could also feel him, and his words cut deeper into my soul. The task that was as mundane a task as you could possibly imagine was really just a reflection on life; a series of boring, repetitive things, things that could often be burdensome or meaningful depending on how one decided to engage with them.

Reflection for the Reader

Do you remember a task that was so repetitive or mundane that it was worthless? Have you ever been overwhelmed in life, wondering if it meant anything at all?

The sacred mundane is the small, everyday actions that are also the profound transformations.

They and their teachings showed us that the simplest things can become sacred. Adira showed me grounding strength, Ishani showed me compassion, Sarthak showed me courage, Vyom showed me creative energy, Kapeesh showed me discernment, and Varya showed me introspection, all of which taught me how presence shifts the mundane to the sacred. It brought me back to the fact that a lot of the weight we carry isn't even physical, it's mental, it's emotional, it's spiritual.

> *As you navigate your own buckets—whether they are literal or metaphorical—pause to ask yourself: What's my process? Am I resisting it, or am I with the flow?*
>
> *You might be surprised at the answers. And from those answers, just maybe you will create a bridge, not just toward the work but towards yourself.*

Moving Stones

The sun climbed higher, the air warmed as the mountains and the chore of fetching water came to an end. Aching body, but the act of carrying the bucket over and over had lulled me into a strange sense of peace—the quiet understanding that surrendering to the simplicity of a task of mundane repetition gives infinitely more power than coddling endless expectations.

Rudra approached me again and I was ready to rest. This time he held his palm out, upward. He said, his tone filled with gentleness and without question of purpose.

"More work?" I asked half jokingly, half dreadfully.

A faint glimmer of amusement glistened across his face as he smiled. He just replied enigmatically saying 'You'll see'.

Not long from the cave, Rudra took me to a clearing. In its center was a stack of stones—some of them small and smooth stones; others large and rugged stones. Across from those there was another pile though smaller, the same wide variety of shapes and sizes.

'Rudra gestured towards the larger pile and said 'I want you to move these stones.' "Take one by one, get them from here and should put them there." He nodded towards the smaller pile of wood.

I stared at him, incredulous. "That's it? 'Just move rocks from one pile to another?'"

He confirmed, 'That's it' with his expression calm and steady.

"But why?" I said, with a hint of frustration in my voice.

He didn't answer. So, instead, he crossed his arms and stepped back. But he wouldn't speak, instead, the clear only path forward was to start.

With a sigh, I sat down, picked up a stone, and carried it to the smaller pile. Sarthak was observing this from a faraway place where he said in quiet strength 'Every time you raise a stone; you don't just strengthen your body but also your spirit.' Every single step forward—because that is all it is—brings courage." But it didn't count as heavy, the act was absurd in its simple scale. I returned to the large pile and picked up another stone, the frustration now growing.

By the tenth stone, I was starting to run questions and complaints through my mind. Why was I doing this? What was the point? This wasn't enlightenment, it was manual labor!

I looked over at Rudra. Still standing on the edge of the clearing, his stare unwavering. It wasn't like he was looking at me directly, but he was there and I felt him as though he were watching not my action, but my inner state.

But that monotony of the work was actually starting to bother me and not just physically. Every time I had to take a stone off the giant pile and carry it into the smaller one, I felt a wave of resistance.

Why don't he tell me?

What was I meant to learn?

I continued to wonder how long I would have to keep doing it.

I couldn't help but be frustrated, all the questions in my mind where the questions just kept circling. I slowed my pace, and my movement grew heavier, not from exhaustion, but from my own weight of resistance.

A Shift

After an eternity of moving stones, I stopped at some point. I dropped the stone in my hand and sat on the grass with my head in my hands.

"I can't… I don't know why, but I can't," I whispered to myself instead of to Rudra.

But Rudra heard me. Quietly he approached, sat down beside me; his presence solidifying. He asked, what can't you do?

I pointed to the piles of stones. "It's meaningless. "I don't get the point," I said.

Rudra said nothing, allowing my words to linger. "What are you resisting?" he said.

I frowned, confused. "I'm not resisting. I'm just… frustrated. There's no purpose to this."

He questioned gently, "Is it the task to which there is no use, or is it that you need to live, and you don't find it?"

His words knocked me like a thunderclap. I was gazing at him, trying to work out what he had just said.

Was the meaningless task my task, or was it my inability to accept and move on from that the meaningless task had no significance outside of my own need to assign significance? Kapeesh, who had been watching, said, "It isn't about meaning, it's about discernment." "The rest fall away, see what truly matters."

His tone patient, Rudra continued. There are limitless tasks like this in life—small, repetitive actions that seem to go nowhere. But is it the action, or how you act upon it?"

I looked back over my shoulder at the pile of stones as if my perception had shifted. The task didn't change, but I had.

Finding Flow

Now as I stood up, it wasn't from frustration, but from curiosity. I picked up another stone and found its weight, its texture, its imperfections. I released the want to rush, the want to question, to carry on back to the smaller pile.

I simply moved the stone.

On each trip, I tuned into the act more and more. The loud crunch of the grass beneath my shoes, the stones settling into the pile, my breathing all of it fell into place. A dance, a flow.

Earlier the resistance had eaten at me, but it now washed away and replaced by a calm focus. The task was the same, but it lacked meaning. It had stopped being because of stones; it was because I put myself present in the act of moving stones.

The sun was dipping lower and lower and Rudra approached me again. He asked, 'What have you learned?'

The stone in my hand felt lighter than it had before; I paused. "I think…" I paused; I tried to find just what I should say. 'That I think has taught me that the meaning in the task isn't something the task itself gives you,' he says. In other words, it's something you bring to the task.

Rudra nodded, a sort of grin on his lips. "And?"

Besides, there was no resistance in the stones and the chore—there was the resistance in me. I just didn't get it, and I was fighting it. However, once I let go of that need to understand, it became… peaceful."

"Exactly," Rudra said. "The stones are a mirror, aren't they, Cherag?" They show you what you bring back to them. You have frustration, impatience, presence, peace, all within you. The stage is the task."

> ## Reflection for the Reader
>
> *Have you seen a task that was mundane or pointless, that served no higher purpose? How did you approach it?*
>
> *Moving stones, I learned, is an act, not one with eternal meaning, but one that we choose to accept as such. Life is filled with these moments: I'll use these moments for washing dishes, folding laundry, and answering emails. Or, they're burdens, or opportunities to be mindful and present.*
>
> *The task isn't providing what you should do with it— it's showing you what you should bring to it. As you navigate the sacred mundane in your own life, pause to reflect: Am I resisting this moment, or am I freeing myself from it? Which do I look for meaning outside of myself, or make it within?*
>
> *The stones, the water, the tasks, everything's a mirror. It's up to you what they reflect.*

Completing the Circle

Instead, the next day I stepped out into the cave and felt the chill of the mountain. During the night the fire in the central pit had burned low, but its embers shone dully. Quietly the monks hushed and walked about just as serene as ever. Stillness and life outside the world somehow balanced each other out — everything felt calm and dynamic, a mirror to what I had been learning.

    When the first fingers of sunlight started to put pink and garnet shades on the peaks, the god of destruction always came to watch the rising of the sun. The same depth of his eyes, but always softer in his gaze, I felt like he saw something in me that wasn't the same anymore.

"Today — we complete the work that you've started," he began.

Returning to the Water

I followed Rudra back to the riverbank, where we'd spent hours carrying water buckets. The tedious task that had once been, was now familiar, even comforting.

I looked at the line of empty buckets, waiting to be filled. "Are we doing this again?" I asked with a smile. Offered a quiet observation Varya, who was standing nearby. She said, "The task is a mirror." It's presence or resistance reflected in each bucket. Look inward."

Rudra also nodded but his face broke into a thin flicker of amusement. 'Yes, but examine now what's different, not in the task, but in you.'

I sat by the river and filled the first bucket. The flow over my hands was constant and rhythmic, the cool water rushed over them. When I picked up the bucket and carried it back to its place, I knew right away.

The water carrying wasn't any different, it was still the task. My approach, my presence, it had transformed, but. The weight of frustration, the requirement for an answer had left me. I found I didn't move with any strain, but smoothly, concentrating on the moment—how the bucket's handle felt, the splash of water with every step, the sunlight of what I now think of as 'purple dawn' flare and play on the surface of the water.

I was tired by the time I had carried the final bucket but my mind was clear and even energized.

As I sat, Rudra walked over from a distance and urged me over to the river. He asked, "What have you learned this time?"

The sound of the river filled the silence, and I thought for a moment. Slowly, I said, "The task doesn't define the experience." It is the presence you bring to it that is the meaning. "When I stopped asking myself to fight this box, I found peace in it," he said.

A quiet smile touched Rudra's lips; he nodded. Just as it is with life, he said. Every day, every repetition, every so-called insignificant act—they are all ways to practice presence, to engage with the current flow of daily existence.

Back to the Stones

We came back to the clearing with the stones after the buckets. Those two piles, that was how I had left them, a proof of my prior work.

"Again," Rudra ordered his voice steady but firm.

"Again?" I asked, surprised. "I had the lesson down."

Rudra held his expression. "It is impossible to exercise your brain to the point of stopping learning."

Taking another deep breath, I got down on one knee and picked up the first stone. It felt different now to move it from one pile to the next, but not about the rocks, it was about the movement, the focus, the rhythm of the task now.

I found myself getting into a meditative state, as I picked stone after stone. His high energy lit up the room as Vyom approached. "Every stone you move is birth," he said. "Everything you do in the world displays your inner and outer worlds." It was the sound of the rocks on top of you, the sound of gravel grinding beneath your shoes, feeling the shifting balance with each rock you placed. It was all music set as part of a large dance with your moment.

This time around, I wasn't questioning the purpose. I wasn't searching for meaning or putting up a fight against simplicity. I was moving stones and was fully in every moment.

The Revelation

Rudra motioned for me to sit next to him when the final stone had been placed. Now the piles of rocks stood perfectly in balance like they had always meant to be.

His voice was low and deliberate as Rudra spoke. "They are not just – the stones, the water," they are no mere tasks. "They are reflections," said Rudra. 'Stillness. Adira reminds you of the strength.' "You show compassion, even for yourself," says Ishani. Sarthak teaches you to carry the heavy loads of life. Kapeesh shows you what's important in every act, Vyom illuminates everything from creation to the mundane, and Varya helps you to reflect on the meaning within everything. This reveals a balance—of harmony between movement and stillness, action and reflection, effort and surrender.

We went back and forth and as I listened, I felt as clear as day. All those things that once seemed so meaningless now were profound teachings in disguise whose simplicity was the door to greater knowing.

As I sat by the fire with the monks that night, I pondered over the journey so far. Rudra's tasks for me weren't arbitrary; they were deliberate, they would pull away each layer of resistance I had left until I could look at myself.

These repetitive actions also forced me to look at how impatient I was, how much I needed to control, and how I would seek meaning outside myself. In the process, they had allowed something more powerful to enter—an understanding we were connected, and simply there, at peace with no expectation.

And I thought about how seldom we pause to acknowledge the mundane elements of our lives. Chores and routines get shuffled through like so many of other things do. What if those moments, that we see as unimportant, are the most sacred? What if they are the key to the stillness we seek?

> ### Reflection for the Reader
>
> *Have you ever had a battle with drudgery, rising up against the drab, wishing that the world was just a bit more thrilling, a bit more meaningful? Do you ever have to mark something (whether it be a simple task or not), as important because you later find out it has something important to tell you?*
>
> *This is an invitation to see those moments in the Sacred Mundane. But the repetitive tasks, the quiet routines, the small acts... There are no obstacles to be overcome. They are mirrors reflecting back to us our inner world.*
>
> *The next time you think doing a simple chore doesn't matter, pause. Breathe. Be present. Ask yourself: How much of my own am I bringing to this space? So, what is it teaching me in return?*
>
> *The lesson is always there, we just don't see it. All we have to do is show up.*

A New Perspective

That night as the fire went out, I was grateful for the water, the rocks, the silence, and the monks who led me through it all. These were no longer tasks; they were teachings and they had burned their mark on my heart.

    Thoughts broke through, my thoughts to be specific and the voice of Rudra suddenly materialized in soft and still words. Rudra said as if he could read my mind, 'The mundane is not separate from the sacred. 'It is the connecting link between the two.' They had wisdom in those tasks: stability, compassion, courage, creation, discernment, introspection, one with each breath. They together guide you toward surrender."

I nodded, realizing something I hadn't understood before. They weren't taking me somewhere else – the tasks, the journey, the lessons. I could feel them bringing me back to me.

In that realization, there was the removal of the weight of the world, and the replacement of it with something I had never known I was searching for: peace.

CHAPTER 8

INTO THE CURRENT

The Reluctance

Rudra took me down to the riverbank and the sun was just starting to rise. The breaths crystallized in the still air, chilled sharp, icy with the morning. In front of us, the Ganga roared, its currents untamed and wild, it was nothing like the mountain portrayed in its behind.

In a crisp voice, Rudra said, 'Today, you'll meet the river.'

The water was churning with an almost hypnotic intense fury, and I stared at the surface. Just thinking about it sent a chill up my spine that had nothing to do with the cold.

"You mean... get in?" I already knew what the answer would be, but I asked hesitantly nonetheless.

Rudra looked at me blankly. He said that the Ganga is more than a river. "It's a force, a teacher. And it will teach you today, as words cannot."

I shifted my feet, suddenly acutely aware of such a great moment. The river coursed on, it flowed, it mercilessly streamed along. How can something so beautiful also be something so threatening?

"Is this really necessary?" I asked for a reprieve.

(Rudra smiled small enigmatic) He replied 'what you resist most is usually what you need most'.

His words smashed through me like a pebble in still water, creating ripples that disturbed the water's surface. I wanted to fight, to yell at him that I wasn't ready, that this wasn't the lesson I wanted to learn. I knew I was resistant, and deep down I knew that resistance wouldn't get me anywhere.

"Why now?" My voice was desperate as I pressed.

He looked at me only, his gaze steady, like he was still up to the task of turning my world inside out. "Because the river is ready for you." "Because you are ready for it."

I wasn't convinced. I feared about plunging into icy, turbulent water. Rudra stood unflappable, leaving little room for debate, however.

The Edge

I walked slowly to the riverbank with hesitance. As I moved closer, the roar of the water grew, until finally filling my ears and silencing the noises of the forest around us. I knelt down and stuck my fingers into the current.

I hadn't quite pictured so much cold. Feeling like a thousand tiny needles piercing through my skin, I could remember the river and the way it was leaving me unforgiven.

"How does it feel?" Rudra asked from behind me.

I shook my hand and said, muttered, "Like a million pricks."

"Good," he said. "Try to imagine what it's like to fight it."

I turned to him, confused. "What do you mean?"

"Resistance," he said simply. You fight the current harder, and it feels stronger. But if you surrender..." "The word hung in the air, and he paused in its breath before allowing it to keep breathing as it was meant to, and as he said, ..."You'll find it carries you."

And I stood there for what felt like an eternity staring at the water. In my mind battled doubts and fears. What if I got swept away by the current? If I couldn't handle the cold what then? What if I wasn't strong enough at all?

As always, Rudra said nothing. A few feet away stood his solid, grounding presence. He wasn't going to push me into taking a snap yet. This was my decision to make.

I took a deep breath and went on. It was too chilly, lapping at my feet, shocking me with its intensity. I wanted to pull back, to retreat from the safety of the dry ground.

Still, Adira's voice hummed softly, as always, her presence the sound to ground my hesitation. "Stay," she said. If you let the river show you, its wisdom. Let it teach you."

I told myself to stay and step again. The water had risen to my ankles, then my shins, every inch of itself a struggle against the cold. In shallow gasps I breathed, my body screaming at me to retreat.

I was shaking not from the cold, but by the time the water was up to my knees I was shaking by the effort of keeping my feet where they were. It pulled at me with a force that was somehow personal like the river knew I had to be up to something or it was trying to make me feel something.

"Breathe," Rudra called out. "Slow, deep breaths."

It was nearly impossible, I tried. The water encased me and with every breath, it felt as if I was struggling, and my chest became tighter.

'Compassion begins with yourself,' Ishani said gently. "Breathe with the river. 'The harder it will feel, the more you resist."

Every muscle in my body was taut as I clenched my fists. The river clearly wanted to fight me, pulling and dragging me with no regard as to how I could relax.

"I couldn't," I told it through a clenched throat.

'Yes," replied Rudra firmly. "Stop fighting it."

"Trusting the river itself is courage, "Sarthak added, quietly. "Let the river guide you."

The Push

I felt a sudden pressure against my back before I could respond. After a moment or two, I realized – Rudra had pushed me.

His shove hit me hard enough to stumble me into the river. It gripped me with cold water and pulled me under.

I panicked for a moment. I flailed my arms, gasped for breath, and all I could see was cold and chaos.

But then, something shifted.

Amid the chaos, a small, quiet voice within me whispered: Stop.

And so, I did.

I stopped flailing. I stopped fighting. The uncontrollable; I no longer tried to control it.

As I let go, that's when the miracle occurred. The river that I had felt so hostile no more than minutes ago now carried me. The current was no longer an enemy but was a guide, a force that not only held me but kept me moving forward.

The cold was still a bit but no longer unbearable, my back floated. I breathed more easily now, slowly, deeply in time with the water.

The sky went on forever upwards, and I knew I was just so small; my fears could not possibly be anything but both. The river roared a steady unblinking melody, its rhythm not to be broken.

I finally understood what Rudra meant at that moment. Surrender wasn't the same as quitting. And it wasn't weakness or defeat. The running was less about exerting myself than it was about losing myself, handing it all over to the river, losing my responsibility for the journey, trusting that the river wouldn't be too wild, that I wouldn't run too far, and that I wouldn't get lost. It was about trust.

After the current finally started to slow down, I was the nearest to the river bank. My mind was so focused, so focused that I could think; all while my body was numb.

His expression as calm as ever waited Rudra for me. He didn't ask me how I felt or what I had learned. He didn't need to.

He didn't say anything like that, he just said, "Now you get it. The river does not take away—it gives. It carries, it transforms, it returns"

I nodded, trying to orient myself. At least, I was beginning to understand.

More in those few minutes than words could ever teach me, was the river. It had demonstrated the magic of surrender, the grace of release, and the power of trusting the current.

I felt there was much to be grateful for: the river, Rudra, and, in some strange way, the lesson I hadn't known I needed.

The Lesson of the Ganga

It was quiet again on the walk back to the cave, gravel crunching under our feet, and the far away roar of the river. My clothes were wet and clung to me but my mind, the pure white inside of me, was lighter than I remembered it being in years. The mess of the Ganga had somehow unwound something inside me, and yet I knew there was more to the lesson.

After we arrived at the cave Rudra motioned for me to sit by the fire. There were just the three of us – the two of us and of course the monks ... None of them to be seen. He gave me a thick woolen shawl that I wrapped tightly around myself, glad of the warmth.

After some time passed, Rudra broke the silence with a voice. "You're not the first to resist the river." "And you won't be the last."

I waited for him to continue and I looked at him.

"It [the Ganga] is a reflection," he said. It's showing you what you are still holding onto, what you are still afraid to release. It's the more it reflects your struggle; the harder you fight it."

His words settled over me, like a second layer of warmth and I nodded slowly.

"I thought control was strength," I admitted, 'for so long.'" I thought holding on was a strength, I could handle anything if only I just tried hard enough. But in the river…" I searched for the right words, pausing. In the river, I realized how futile it was. All that fighting, that struggle… it just made me struggle more."

Rudra smiled faintly. 'Control is an illusion,' he said. "Life doesn't flow because of our will, but because of it." Recognizing when it's time to let go is how you know you're strong."

His words struck me like a wave, there was no denying the truth to them. How many times had I held onto something — an identity; a plan; a fear — thinking it would provide me with stability? How many times did that very clinging make me suffer the most?

'The river didn't weaken you,' Rudra went on. "It revealed you. It showed you what is there, under the layers of resistance and fear."

I closed my eyes and relived the instant that I had thrown in the towel. There had not been fear in that instant, no doubt — only trust. Nowhere was it the absence of challenge, it was the acceptance of it.

The Illusion of Certainty

"Why can't I just let go of things?" Barely above a whisper, I asked.

A small branch was fed into the fire by Rudra who leaned forward. He said it was "because we confuse certainty with security." So, we think if we can dictate the outcome, we'll be okay. 'Life doesn't work that way,' but…"

Towards the flickering flames, he pointed. "Look at the fire. It burns only when there is balance — fuel, oxygen, and heat. Take away one element, and it extinguishes. Still, it neither holds wood, nor resists the wind. 'But it's just a simple thing that lives hand in hand with what is.'"

I had watched the flames dance, wild and deliberate. The fire wasn't fighting to burn, it was just doing its thing.

Ganga is the lesson, Rudra said. Surrendering is not giving up." For it's to sync yourself up to the flow of life and know life will take you where you need to go."

The Ripple Effect

Days went on and Rudra's words didn't leave my head. But the monks themselves seemed to be embodied with this principle of surrender. It was deliberate, yet not one action was rushed, almost as if every second had its own holy cadence.

I did see one morning a monk take water from a bucket to water small plants by the cave. But he didn't hurry through it. He didn't waste a single drop. The act was simple but its grace was profound.

Rudra noticed my stare and said, "That's surrender."

"Oh, I can tell already," Vyom said, his voice gleaming with vitality, "Your every action molds your world." 'There is creation even in surrender.'

His words put the river into my words. The Ganga had a purpose, even in its chaos. It did not hesitate on its path, but just flowed and carved out its way through the mountains, feeding all that was behind it.

I began to view surrender as a lifestyle, not as a one-time thing. But it was about the way in which I would tackle each task, each challenge, each encounter. The most helpful part was being able to be present — to trust that whatever the next step was, I would know when it was ready.

On one evening as the sun set over the horizon, I could be seen by myself, standing alongside the bank of a river. The water was calmer now, the echoes of its powerful current were faded, but it was still water.

I knelt down and my fingers raked through the icy flow. I remember being pushed in the river with the fear I felt at that time.

Rudra stood next to me, as if he'd appeared in response to my thoughts, saying: "Fear doesn't go away." You don't beat depression; you befriend it."

I looked at him, surprised by his words. "Befriend it?"

He nodded. "Fear is a messenger. This shows you where you are clinging, where you are resisting. But instead of pushing it away, invite it in and ask it 'what is it trying to teach me?"

Varya talked steadily, like the river itself; "Sit with it," she said. "Wisdom is the wisdom of fear, provided that you have the patience to hear."

The river's flow sang in the background, I let his words seep in. I had always had a fear, and it ran in my blood to overcome it. But what if it was a guide? What if, like the river, it had more of a purpose in mind?

Weeks turned into days and I started to see a change in me. The lessons of the Ganga weren't of today or tomorrow: they wouldn't anchor merely at the riverbank. The lessons were as constant as humanity.

I became ready to let go of wanting control and open myself up to what might come. The silence of the caves made me confront parts of myself I had long been adept at ignoring, my fears, doubts, and vulnerabilities.

In every wanting, there is a limiting belief, and it is our limiting beliefs that get us, but instead of being overwhelmed by them, I found strength in acknowledging and embracing them. I worked on sitting with the pain, allowing it to move through me, just like the current of the river.

And in doing so, I discovered something unexpected: **freedom**.

Surrender was giving up nowhere near what it would have been if I had been chasing money or success…it was giving up the parts of me that I had buried under the weight of resistance. This time it was all about trusting the journey, knowing where the destination was but not knowing how to get there.

Reflection for the Reader

So here you sit with me, thinking about your relationship to surrender as I sit here writing these words.

What are you still holding on to that doesn't serve you anymore? What fears are holding you back from stepping into the current of your life?

Surrender isn't a weakness; I learned from the Ganga—it's a strength. Ishani taught me compassion, Adira grounded me, Sarthak taught me courage, Vyom revealed creation in surrender, and we discussed Varya guiding me back into myself, to reflect on fear's lessons. Along with me, they helped me to come to a greater awareness of the flow of the river.

So, I ask you: How would surrendering look in your life? How can he trust the river, the fire, or the journey?

The deep lessons are sometimes learned outside the stillness, as I've learned in the current. When you let go, you might just discover that the river knows where it's supposed to take you.

CHAPTER 9

THREE REALIZATIONS

The Unveiling of Ego

The morning air bit sharp in the mountains—the kind of cold that fills your lungs like a gift from the world, clean and unspoiled. The cave entrance had me sitting inside, my body wrapped within a woolen shawl, as the world outside sat wrapped in silence, interrupted perhaps only by the distant gurgle of the Ganga. The monks gracefully moved about in the characteristic way with deliberate yet unhurried action.

I had started to see how much of that time was taken up resisting, either the physical discomfort of the cold, the monotony of tasks, or the silence that brings me face to face with my thoughts. Resistance was a reflex now, more or less, something that I hadn't even noticed I had come to resist.

He came quietly, making almost no sound on rocks. He handed me a steaming cup of water; its warmth actually soothed my hands. She steps forward, Ishani, the scene serene. "That's the silence you feel, not emptiness but a doorway, and you're invited to step deeper into yourself," she whispered.

Rudra spoke quietly but with a tone that suggested he knew what was going on almost as well as you did. "You are restless this morning."

I didn't quite know what to say to him. "I feel... exposed," I said. "None of that's been an issue here. This place, this silence It's making me look at parts of myself that I didn't even know existed."

He nodded ever so slightly before a faint smile dragged itself onto the corners of his lips. But the mountains have a way of doing that. 'Nothing but the truth' is all they strip away the noise to leave you with."

The steam coiled upwards with the offering of silence; I stared into the cup. "But if the truth was something I didn't want to see?"

Rudra gestured for me to join with him. So, we walked and, eventually, found a flat rock overlooking the valley, the Ganga looking glint and glorious far down below. He motioned toward me to sit and sat beside me as well.

He started by asking, not demanding, "Tell me, what do you see when you look at yourself?"

I was caught off guard by the question. I said slowly, 'I'm not sure.' "Yeah, I just see someone trying to make sense, make some sense out of it."

He pressed, 'And beneath that?'

I frowned and didn't know where this was going. "I see below that someone's scared of letting people down. A person who doesn't want to lose control."

Rudra nodded, glaring blankly. "That is your ego talking," he said.

I hadn't expected that word to land with a weight. Ego. I had read about it, I had heard about it, it wasn't a new concept to me, even though I understood. Hearing it here, now though, made it seem different.

Rudra went on: "Ego isn't simply pride or arrogance." It's a false self that you ship yourself into the world for protection. The voice that says I am this, I am that – that is not who you are."

His words struck a chord. I started thinking about how much of my identity hinged on external markers – my job, my accomplishments, my roles in my family and in society. Losing this job didn't feel like losing myself, maybe what I lost wasn't me.

Ego as a Mask

"Understanding the ego is a mask is the first step to awakening," Rudra said. 'It's not who you are, it's who you think you need to be."

'The mask shields you, but it also clouds the radiance of your true self,' Adira piped up nearby as Rudra spoke. Throw it away if you have the strength. Then let yourself feel the strength beneath the mask."

Three Realizations

There's no way I could forget their words. Their truth was unsettling but it was undeniable. How many times had I clung to that mask because I was scared of what lay beneath it? How many times had I allowed it to become my worth?

Rudra's eyes scanned the horizon. 'Ego isn't inherently bad,' he said. "You can use it as a tool, as a way to orient to the world." 'When you let it take over. When you stop seeing the mask as a mask, and you start to believe that's actually your face, that's when it becomes a prison."

A memory came back, to one of the first days after I had lost my job. It was a shame that feasted on my soul and wouldn't allow me to face even the smallest people and the smallest interactions from a place other than a complete failure. I had always thought without my title, my achievements, without those things I was nothing.

Rudra added as if he could feel my thoughts, "Letting go of the ego doesn't mean losing yourself." "When you hear it, it means finding the self that isn't the labels, the roles."

When the temperature rose, the sun's heat beginning to thaw the morning frost, Rudra turned to me with such a question that made its way through layer after layer of pretense.

He asked me, 'Whose expectations are you living for?'

The reaction struck me like a sudden blow. I started to say something, but couldn't. Whose expectations? Whose was it? My parents, my colleagues, society? Was it his guilt, or mine – building out of so many years of trying to prove myself?

"Living for others' expectations is a giving up of your power when you do that," Rudra continued, his tone gentle but strong, like someone who had been down this road and wanted to stop you from going down it. The actions you take? Are from your ego, not because it translates to you and not because it serves you but because 'it strives for approval'."

I looked back on all of those times I had pursued goals that meant nothing to me and poured all of myself into it for validation, even if I knew in the back of my head it wasn't going to make me happy. It was like putting a mirror in front of my soul, revealing truths I had kept from myself for a long time.

The Unveiling

Rudra stood, brushing the dust off his robes; he gestured for me to follow. Silence filled the air, and we walked back to the cave.

Inside monks were gathered in their usual quiet circle; their presence had grounded. Rudra took his spot among them and motioned for me to sit too.

Breaking the silence, he said: "'The ego isn't something you conquer.' You get it. It's something you understand. That is, only then can you decide when to wear the mask and when to take it off."

The lesson sank in and I nodded. No, the enemy wasn't the ego; it was a part of me, yet it also belonged to me. The first step to freedom, to live authentically was recognizing it.

The fire crackled quietly and I felt a transition happening. It hadn't been an epiphany or turning point. The understanding was quiet, a simple powerful realization that I was starting to see myself.

But this journey was far from over and for the first time ever I felt as if I were among the things I should, not turning my back on myself but my back to the truth of who I was.

Pain as a Path

The cave walls flinched from the flickering shadows of the softly crackling fire. The monks sat there, awaiting in their usual serene silence, grounding as always. Rudra had been talking about the ego, stripping it down, layer by layer to expose the cruel lies it had ever promised. His words sank in, but another question took over that was more like a feeling in my stomach.

"What about pain?" Breaking the silence, I asked. The cavern echoed out my voice faintly. "What do we do with it? "What are we supposed to do with it, not let it destroy us?"

Rudra looked at me then, his eyes piercing my soul… and stretching over lifetimes. He said nothing for a moment, are the answer was maybe in the silence itself.

He spoke, his voice quiet but even, "Pain isn't something to escape from. It is something to enter." Sarthak sat quietly, adding, "To enter into pain is an act of **courage**." Each step into it makes your spirit stronger."

It was something within me that the words landed on so heavy. My whole life had been spent trying to avoid, or try to numb, or push away pain. Unwelcome, an intruder, a guest unwelcomed enough to spend years trying to keep out.

Rudra inched forward a bit, his tone gentle but more insistent. "Pain is not your enemy. It is your teacher. It reveals where you've got wounded, where you cling too tightly, and where you have to let go."

In my mind, I traveled back to the months that followed me losing my job. That loss hurt like I couldn't even begin to explain, it was suffocating, an ache that would not turn away. I blamed the world, I blamed myself, I blamed anything and everything that I could put the anguish on. Unfortunately, I had to do that because I was only prolonging it and allowing it to fester rather than heal.

"You can't heal what you don't face," Rudra continued. "Pain demands to be heard, it demands that it has to be felt. And only then it can teach you what it was meant to, thus build the path for you."

The Lesson of the Flame

Rudra picked up a small bowl of water and put it over the fire. But the heat quickly heated the water into steam, puffs of it growing and fading into the air.

"Pain, like fire," he said, pointing to the bowl. The worst of it is, if it's left unchecked, it can consume you. To burn, to transform is different if you let it. It becomes fuel." Like fire refining gold, pain takes away what's superficial and leaves you with what's lasting in you – who you really are.

The analogy struck a chord. The fire wasn't destructive in its essence; the same went for pain. It could annihilate, yes, but it could also annihilate like the sun, burn apart like a star, purify like a crucible, illuminate like a flash bulb, transform like grass first blackened then transmuted to gold. It was a choice of how to go about it and how to keep it.

"Have you ever had your pain?" His question was simple, piercing.

The truth was too ugly to admit, and I hesitated. I had buried my pain for so much of my life, numbing it with distraction, burying it under layers of activity and denial.

He said, as if he'd read my thoughts, "Most people don't." It is a reason they run from it, they suppress it or lash out because of it. Pain doesn't go away when you wish you could ignore it. It waits. And it waits for you to be ready."

I remembered the lessons the monks had subtly sublimated through their silence upon the words of Rudra. The pain didn't scare them; they sat in it and let it flow through them like a wave.

Rudra answered with a voice that resonated with all the breeze as it rose and floated upright, "The second realization is that pain is a path." The destination is not the destination, it is a very important component of reaching the destination.

It seemed liberating, but also scary. Pain wasn't something to overcome or to shy away from, it was a companion with a point to show me that I may otherwise not have found.

I remembered the discomfort of each moment on this journey—the freezing waters of the Ganga, the grueling climb up the mountains, the minds deadening repetition of and nothing else. All of those moments were a little bit painful, but they were also a little bit growing.

The Mirror of the Ganga

Rudra waved me to follow him. We stepped outside the cave, together. Mountain air crisp, wrapped around us like a shawl. Below the Ganga flowed, its surface shimmering under the pale light of the moon.

Rudra looked into the river, his voice contemplative. It flows freely, though warring does not let it flow without obstacles. Its course is shaped by rocks, currents, rapids, but nothing impedes its path. In fact, it is because of them that it becomes what it is. "The river dances with the rocks," he said, his stillness masking his vibrancy. I said, you need the obstacles, otherwise there is no song."

I looked at the river and watched its endless motion, the motion of something eternal. I realized these rocks and currents were like pain. It formed the course of life, making a way, where no way was before.

Rudra continued, "The river doesn't resist." It doesn't struggle against rocks or circumnavigate them. They let them be part of its journey and move through them, around them."

It was a metaphor that stuck. How many times have I turned away from the rocks in my own path and set traps for them, never seeing how they are a part of the whole?

So, Rudra and I stood watching the river, and he looked at me and asked me what most would consider a simple, albeit profound, question.

"Cherag, what are you holding onto?"

I was caught off guard by the question. The things I had gripped onto—my job, my identity, my need for control—rolled through my mind. There was, but something that ran deeper, something personal.

I admitted, the words barely audible, 'My pain.' The pain I've been holding onto.

Rudra nodded, understanding the expression on his face. "Pain can be a comfort," he said. "It's familiar – not because it feels good." "To let it go is to step into the unknown."

The first 'mind to matters' is to reorganize our entire foundation; no longer confined to the physical structure of our physical bodies, but changing entirely our perception and programming. Letting it go means stepping into the unknown."

The truth of his words hit me and I felt a lump rise in my throat. In order to let go of pain, I had to let go of the stories that surrounded it, of the identity that it had influenced me to embody.

The Healing in Surrender

"Pain is not you," Rudra said, softly. "It's something you go through. But it is not you."

It was a realization: it was like a weight lifting; it felt like a crack in my armor. I decided to sit with my pain honestly for the first time: not to analyze it, not to fix it, just to feel it.

Life continued as well, on its regular bearing forward. It's not that pain is the destination, it's that it is the path, and if you let it be, it can be your transformation.

The warmth of the fire embracing us on our return, and of a quiet release overtook me. The pain I had carried for so long weighed nothing on me. It was like a teacher, one that had been waiting for me to hear, for so long.

It was far from over, but not for the first time the journey of pain felt that I was ready to walk it, no longer with resistance, but with acceptance.

The Present Moment

The fire in the cave had burned low and glowed softly against the dark stone walls. Their stillness had been an anchor to keep my restless thoughts company and I sat in the circle of monks. The second realization: Pain was a path that changed me somehow.

However, as I started to accept the pain, another question floated around at the back of my mind.

'And present moment? You know you are ok here.' Breaking the silence, I finally asked. They felt like they weighed more than their face value. "How do you live in it? When everything else pulls you away, how do you stay here?

He looked up at Rudra from the fire, he didn't seem like there was anything meaningful on his mind. He said his voice was quiet but firm: "The present moment is the only reality." "There is no finding of it; there is a returning to it."

For much of my life, I had been caught between two forces: the heaviness of this past, and the lightness of that unknown future. They were past, they carried regrets and mistakes and stories I couldn't shake off. The future was full of unanswered questions, expected responses, and endless 'what-ifs.'

Rudra continued, "The past is a memory and the future is a projection." And neither exists except in your mind. "This moment, this moment right now – there is no other moment—this is the only reality, the only thing you have."

I tried to imagine how many hours I had spent focusing on the past: things I couldn't undo, conversations I wanted to go back to and change. It continued on with the loops of the future; planning, worrying, and wanting something too far away.

"'You cannot live in the past or the future," Rudra said. And you can only think about them. To live is to be present."

Softly the fire crackled and the monks were silent, making Rudra's words echo all around.

The third realization, he said, is that all that exists is the moment now. "That's the very gate to peace, clarity, truth."

The statement was simple but deep. The present moment wasn't just a concept, it was a practice, it was a discipline, it was a way of being.

Rudra continued, "When you do resist the present, you'll suffer. You hang on to what was and stretch for what could be, and in doing so, you pass right by the life that's happening right before you."

I knew he was telling the truth in my chest somehow, a resonance so true and deep I couldn't deny it. How many times had I let a moment pass me by for something else? How many times had I let the now go by while I was too busy not noticing it?

I followed him outside the cave once more, as Rudra motioned for me to. Its rhythm was steady and unchanging and the Ganga flowed below.

Rudra said only: "Watch the river. It won't cling to the rocks it passes by; it won't rush to the ocean. It is fully present every step of its journey flowing."

The water's surface reflected the pale light of the moon, and I watched. The river didn't fight, didn't struggle.

"We know to be present," Rudra added. "It's to let go of what we've passed and trust that the future will arrive in its time. All we have to do is flow."

It hit me that that was a metaphor. Life seemed like the river — stop for a moment it was frozen, a journey you could only experience in the present.

Anchoring in the Present

I turned to see Rudra, his gaze was steady. "Close your eyes," he said. "Breathe." Encouraged, her voice a soothing balm, Ishani said, 'Let your breath guide you home to yourself.' It's a phrase that feels like; Each moment is a gift waiting to be unwrapped."

I listened, letting my eyes close, and focused on my breath. Inhale. Exhale. Through the simple act of breathing, I was anchored away from all my thoughts into the now.

"What do you feel?" His voice, gentler than Rudra, asked.

I paused, a bit not being sure how to respond. However, as I kept breathing, I started to notice things I hadn't before, the coolness of the air against my skin, the steady rise and fall of my chest, the faint scent of earth and fire.

Finally, the words themselves surprised me, "I feel…alive," I said.

Rudra nodded. "That is the power of now. This is enough, and it reminds you that you are alive and you are here."

Rudra's words started to take its meaning as we stood by the river. The present moment was not something to chase or capture, something to surrender to.

"Resistance," Rudra said, "is what keeps you from the present. What it is, you push against it because you want it to be something other than what it is. The moment you let go of that resistance you find peace."

It reminded me of so many ways that I had fought with life, and how I had grappled with it; how I had held onto the past and worried about the future. And each time I resisted, it brought me further away from the now.

Rudra asked, "What would happen if you stopped resisting?" Would you accept this moment for exactly what it is?

The simplicity of the question made it mask its power as a challenge.

A Moment of Surrender

I stood there, with the Ganga running endlessly before me; something changed. I relaxed, I allowed myself to stop fighting, to stop resisting, to stop controlling and to let go.

It was the present moment, as though the river's current flowed over me, washing me whole, and the feeling of peace that I had been unattainably searching for years. It was a presence of peace, a being fully here, being fully alive peace; it wasn't born of answers or certainty.

> ### Reflection for the Reader
>
> *Have you ever actually been present? Or mind and spirit not just in body? This week, have you ever let yourself go and be, instead of embracing the past and future?*
>
> *This present moment is always here for you. In the journey of returning to the present moment, we remind ourselves to start by trusting in Adira's strength, Ishani's compassion, Sarthak's courage, Vyom's creativity, and Varya's introspection. It doesn't demand anything from you, except your undivided attention and your willingness to stop and listen.*
>
> *Try it now. Close your eyes. Breathe. What do you feel? Hear? See? Let them wash over you now, as the river rushes, and what can it teach you?*

A New Beginning

Returning to the cave with Rudra I felt lighter, freer as if I had released a piece of myself which I had no more use for. It wasn't a realization. It was a gift. A gateway to a way of living that simply felt more authentic, more aligned, more true.

The circle of the monks sat around, their stillness a demonstration of what can be obtained from going about together. I belonged here not just to the circle but to the moment, to the journey, to life.

Then the past did not have the same weight as the future. This here, now, was what mattered.

It was far from over, but at least for the first time, I found myself prepared to walk it, one moment at a time.

CHAPTER 10

A GLIMPSE OF INFINITY

The Threshold of the Infinite

The cave's fire was low and embers of it pulsed, with a quiet, slow rhythm that echoed the stillness of monks seated around its fire. I sat cross-legged on my mat, my body was physically present, but my mind was pulled by questions that had no easy answers. Each lesson so far had left me both enlightened and disoriented, as though the foundations of who I thought I was were crumbling to make space for something entirely new.

Rudra's eyes settled on me; his silence profound yet expectant. He said, "Today we are going to go beyond what you are aware of. More than what you think is possible."

His words weren't so empty, it filled the room, the air outside wasn't so light either. I was excited and afraid at the same time. What lay hidden beyond the limits of my perception? How could I step into the unknown, where the mind's need for explanation and justification had to be left behind?

Rudra started mentioning about energy — not something as mystical, but something that powers everything, everything that is life. He mentioned "This energy, flow of life is true for every living being. An energetic flow that connects body, mind and spirit. This energy is located in you, and it can be mapped out on specific points that act as conduits."

He directed me to close my eyes and simply follow his voice. "Feel your breath, and let it guide you inward."

I did as he told me, my breath a thread pulling me into myself. I became aware, slowly, of things I had never felt, before, a gentle warmth in my palms, a faint tingling at the base of my spine, a quiet hum that seemed to vibrate itself through, into, all of my being.

"These are your energy points," Rudra continued, "they are not objects to be located, but experiences to be felt. It is helping you understand yourself and the world around you."

Unlocking the Points

Each energy point in the body had its purpose, Rudra explained, as a gateway to particular experiences of human life. "If you are balanced and aligned in these points," he said, "you will feel the harmony. When they are blocked or are ignored, dissonance results…"

These points he didn't speak of in esoteric terms but had to do with the practical pathways that were intimately tied together with the physical body's patterns. He continued, "They are like rivers present in your being, flowing through you. Life is great when the rivers flow freely. Stagnation sets in when they are obstructed."

I found his analogy profoundly simple yet surprisingly powerful. For the first time I could see these rivers within me, rivers of vitality, rivers of awareness flowing through every part of me. Yet, I couldn't help but wonder: How many times had I forgotten these rivers and untreated myself to their life-giving flow?

Nevertheless, the monks had begun to guide me through a series of alchemical practices that would awaken these energy points. No chants, no rituals, just intentional movements and breathwork that I have to focus on.

I tried a posture that felt both unfamiliar and strangely comfortable, Rudra told me, "Focus. Let the energy flow through you don't try to control it, just observe it."

It began slowly, the flow which felt warm with a slight vibration. However, the more I practiced, the more aware I became of the energy as something deep and sleepy had just been awakened. Normally my mind was a non-stop chatterbox of my thoughts, but focusing on the energy flow poured a deep, resonant stillness.

So, Rudra explained, "What you are feeling is your connection to the infinite. Always, waiting to be seen. You have to let go of the noise of noise that consumes your awareness to access it though."

As we continued, I found something in me trying to resist myself. My body ached, and my mind started wandering, and the doubts came flooding in. What was I doing? Was this even real?

Rudra understood my difficulty. He calmly said, 'The mind will resist. It is a creature of control, of keeping hold of that which is known. To get to the infinite, we must surrender. You have to let go of need to understand, and just be."

His words resonated, but I couldn't quite let go. It was easier said than done. And every instinct in me grabbed onto something. Demanding an explanation, a framework, a sense that I knew why. However, bringing attention back to breathing and with a deep exhale, I woke up and I felt just the tiniest shift. Resistance had softened and, in its place, there was a tentative openness.

The 33 Energy Points Awakening

The air crackled with anticipation as the seven monks gathered themselves around me, seated cross-legged. Facing me was Rudra, his eyes were peaceful and focused, like he was looking into me and through me, and he could see the energy flowing within me waiting to awaken.

"Today, we are going to awaken the flow of energy in your 33 gateways, the vertebrae of your spine," he started. "Each wisdom fragment has its essence held within each section of the spine, each of us will guide you through their fragment. We will together align the energy to guide you towards a connection with yourself and the infinite. And when we ask stay with your breath and concentrate at the energy point." His voice was steady but charged with purpose. " But to feel the infinite, you must experience it—not as an idea, but as a flow through the gateways of your being. The monks and I will guide you through this." he said.

1. The Coccyx and Sacrum – Stability

Adira stood up, her movements, were slow, yet powerful embodying an unshakable strength, a strength of grounding and inner stability. Her presence reminded me that without stability, there was no flow of energy. Grounding was not just stability; it was the anchor in the chaos. She had the stability aura ... the anchor in the midst of chaos. She bowed slightly and spoke, her voice deep and unwavering. "Your being is built on stability. No structure can rise up if there is no strong base. Our spine begins at the coccyx and sacrum—five vertebrae that anchors you to the earth and to ourselves."

She guided me to focus on the first five vertebrae:

1. Awareness – "Feel the foundation of your being awakened. Awareness is the first step in building stability."
2. Gratitude – "Anchor yourself in appreciation for the life that supports you."
3. Humility – "Strength is born from humility. Embrace your smallness and discover your infinite nature."
4. Clarity – "See clearly the path that lies before you. Clarity strengthens your purpose."
5. Expression – "Express your truth with stability, rooted in who you are."

I visualized energy rising through these points and I felt super grounded – like I'd become a rock, unmovable and unshakeable.

2. The Lumbar Spine – Compassion

Ishani approached with her soothing and empathetic presence nurturing a universal connection like a warm embrace. Her words were gentle. "The lumbar spine is the keeper of energy of compassion, compassion not only for others but for yourself. This is where you will find the vertebrae that will let you move on with love and courage."

We focused on the successive five vertebrae:

6. Surrender – "Let go of resistance. True compassion arises when you surrender to what is."
7. Unity – "Feel the oneness of all life. Compassion bridges the gap between you and the world."
8. Courage – "It takes courage to open your heart, even when it has been hurt."
9. Compassion – "Love flows freely when you connect with the heart of all beings."
10. Resilience – "Compassion requires strength. Resilience allows you to keep loving, even in adversity."

The warmth of his guidance softened my chest, and the energy began to rise, a soft yet powerful energy, like a stream breaking through the stone.

3. The Lower Thoracic Spine - Discernment

Kapeesh moved closer; his eyes sharp with intellect as if he was scraping away all of the hidden truths to reveal my true self just by a fleeting glance. His voice was calm and had weight. "The ability to see what's true and what's illusion is what's termed discernment. This wisdom is held in the lower thoracic vertebrae, guiding you through the 'complexities' of life."

He guided me through the following eight vertebrae:

11. Patience – "Discernment requires patience. Wait for clarity before you act."
12. Empathy – "Understand others deeply to see beyond surface judgments."
13. Forgiveness – "Discernment frees you from the chains of resentment."
14. Discipline – "A disciplined mind can distinguish truth from distraction."
15. Service – "True discernment leads to service, for it sees the interconnectedness of all life."
16. Detachment – "See without attachment. Discernment is impartial."
17. Adaptability – "Flow with life's changes while staying true to your purpose."
18. Harmony – "Discernment brings harmony, aligning you with the rhythms of the universe."

When I focused on these points, my mind felt more apparent, more sharp, more connected to the truths I had been ignoring for all of my life.

4. The Upper Thoracic Spine - Courage

Sarthak was tall and commanding, purposefully brave; he emanated the ability required to conquer fear. He stood beside me and spoke with a resolve that would not waver. "The upper thoracic spine is where courage lives. These vertebrae carry the energy of facing fear, of standing tall even when life challenges you."

Together, we activated the successive five vertebrae:

19. Truth – "Courage begins with truth. Live in alignment with what is real."
20. Stability – "Root yourself firmly. Stability gives rise to fearless action."
21. Creativity – "Courage births creativity, allowing you to envision and build anew."
22. Authenticity – "Be true to yourself, no matter the cost."
23. Trust – "Courage requires trust—in yourself, in others, and in life's flow."

The energy here was violent yet controlled, a flame rising throughout me that consumed all of the fear.

5. The Cervical Spine – Creation

Vyom stepped forward. He emitted a reflective demeanor, one of calming introspection in which he invited me to look inside of me and find out the truths buried inside of me that are ready to be held. With his voice which was calm and carried a sense of wonder said "The cervical spine is the gateway to creation. The energy of infinite possibility flows freely here."

He led me through the seven cervical vertebrae:

24. Prosperity – "Recognize abundance in all forms. Creation thrives in gratitude."

25. Purification – "Cleanse yourself of what no longer serves. Creation requires purity."
26. Flexibility – "Be flexible in your approach. Creation is ever-changing."
27. Energy – "Harness the energy within you to manifest your dreams."
28. Connection – "Creation flows from connection to the universal source."
29. Alignment – "Align your body, mind, and spirit to channel creation effortlessly."
30. Awakening – "Creation awakens the dormant potential within you."

It was like it had me rising toward something larger than I was at this level of energy — it felt light and expansive.

6. The Atlas – Introspection

Her essence, Varya, stepped forth with Her serene and transcendent presence of surrender to the infinite and the universal energy carefree; willingly flowing through. She laid a hand gently on the crown of my head. "The topmost vertebrae is the atlas. It holds the energy of surrender. This here is the end of the journey, and you will rejoin the infinite."

We focused on the last three points:

31. "Integration': 'Bring all aspects of yourself into unity."
32. Ascension – 'Rise to states of consciousness above the material."
33. Bliss – "Surrender fully. But now, right now, you are one with the divine."

It filled me like a river into the ocean dissolving all boundaries and leaving only peace.

He was not just one of the fragments, because Rudra was the thread which united all of them. His wisdom was infinite, no unique, but each energy was connected to the next.

"The wisdom of the fragments has guided you through the 33 gateways. This flow of these energies together creates the flow of life. What I can tell you is that you are not separate from the infinite, you are the infinite."

There was a circle of them, monks around me, with the confidence of the circle unified by strength. I was complete in that moment, aligned, awakened, and whole.

"The energy is now awake, and you flow back into 'A Glimpse of Something More' simply by reflecting on the journey you went on."

But then again, Rudra's final words seemed to sink over me as I felt the energy running through me, not apart from me, but me. It felt like my body was alive, my mind was quiet and my spirit was expansive. The silence deepened and then, as silence does, I felt it—and I know now what it was, a look inside of infinity, no longer a concept, but a fact, a living presence in my body.

A Glimpse of Something More

I felt incredibly light as we carried on like the walls of my body were being stripped away. The cave and the fire, the monks, faded away, and I was overwhelmed by presence. It wasn't an out-of-body experience, it was an in-body, a total presence in every cell, every breath, the sense of me and everything else beginning to melt into one.

"It's OK," Rudra said, his voice soothing me, even though I felt myself spreading. "This is the gateway. This is not a destination, but a portal to what exists outside."

All I could see was something I couldn't put a name to, there for a brief moment only. It wasn't a vision or a thought, but a knowing, an all-knowing, all-understanding of a place, a place I belonged in, yet a place that was vast and timeless, and infinite.

Then, just as fast as it came, it vanished. Opening my eyes, the firelight told me I was in a cave. My breath came shallow, my race palpable, like I had touched something far more than myself, and came back changed.

In silence Rudra allowed me to sit and let the experience settle. The monks didn't move either, their peaceful quiet support.

"With all you experienced is a glimpse of infinity, Rudra said finally." Something we can't hold on to, or analyze. You just have to experience it, so you remember, who you really are."

That night, the cool stone beneath me, I laid down with quiet reverence as I began this journey. It was a substance I didn't really get yet but I had found the thread to the edge of something, something profound, something about unlearning as much as learning.

It wasn't a place, a state to reach. Now, it waited to be noticed here. I was ready to accept it, for the first time.

Surrendering to the Infinite

The embers in the cave were low, their soft glow dimming the rocks of the cave. My heart was alive with a quiet intensity, but my breath was steady as I sat cross-legged. A slight bit of the experience I had lit the edges of my awareness, and I wasn't taking it in, wasn't really aware of it, but it was unmistakably profound. I had somehow kind of realized that the infinite wasn't something you arrived at, it was something you felt, and that happened when the noise within went quiet.

Rudra motioned for me to get up. His voice, however, steadied himself: "We are not done," he said, simply. Infinite isn't only flashes; it has to become part of the very fibers of your being.

The cool night air greeted us as we stepped outside the cave. The stars stretched endlessly above, stark against the velvet darkness. I was certain each seemed like a little reflection of the infinite Rudra referred to.

Taking me down a narrow path toward the Ganga, her faraway roar was calming and commanding. The river was no longer just a body of water; it was a power of nature, movement, surrender, and power. Its flow was never wavering or forced, yet stone cold and unyielding, these are paradoxical powers which we shall refer to as strength and grace.

'Like the mind, Rudra started to speak, 'The river is …' 'It moves and turbs and resists, and also carries. If we are to understand the Infinite, then we must first understand the current that is within you.'

The sound of running water echoed as we entered a clearing by the river's bank, but there the water raced too fiercely for an imaginary feeling, resembling the chaos I felt inside me often. Rudra turned and looked at me with steady gaze. "Sit," he instructed.

I lowered myself onto a flat rock, warmth starting to run through my pants. Deafening in the night the only sound was the roar of the river, so unlike the silence of the cave.

'Now,' said Rudra, 'hear.' It was not to the river. "What do you hear?"

At first, all I could think about was noise – the rush of the water, the howl of the wind against the trees, and the occasional squawk of a faraway bird. Closing my eyes, and breathing to plant my body, I heard a different sound coming into being. It wasn't outside of me.

Rudra said, as if he only read my thoughts: 'That is the current. The Ganga flows through this valley the way it flows through you. You give up to connect to the infinite. You need to surrender to it, not fight it, not control it."

The Act of Surrender

Rudra's words circled through my brain as he talked me through a sequence of breaths. Inhale felt like a collection of energy, exhale a release. The boundaries between my breath and the river's rhythm started to blur slowly. The sound of rushing water had somehow integrated itself, and now when I breathed it seemed as if I was breathing with it, flowing with it.

Suddenly, without wind, Rudra said, 'Stand.'

My resolution was hard but my legs were shaky; I obeyed. He pointed down to the river, the current ice-cold in the starlight. "Step in," he instructed.

Panic surged within me. It took its power too, the way it pulled through the rocks. "It's freezing," I protested.

Rudra's face remained calm. "Exactly. The infinite is not something you can warm yourself in. The infinite is not something comforting, the infinite is raw, unfiltered, and sometimes to the point of being overwhelming. You have to let go of your fear to touch it."

Waves of doubt were passing through my mind. I thought back to the glimpse earlier, the brief moment of true connection that I was wishing for more. Now having understood, was I willing to step back from the edge?

I waded in, taking a deep breath. All of a sudden, my skin was stricken with the coldest sight, the coldest sound, the coldest anything that pricked my skin like a thousand little harpoons. A current pulled me ever so slightly away from where I wanted to remain, and every single instinct in me was telling me to retreat, but I stayed where I was, my breath steadying me.

Rudra called from the bank, 'Feel it!' "Don't resist. Don't fight. Let it move through you."

I shut my eyes, concentrating on them. It wasn't just cold, the water itself flowed with alien force, cleansing and overwhelming. Between the current and the nearby wall, I could feel my body tense painfully against the current, muscles straining to hold their ground.

Rudra's voice barked through the chaos. "Let go." "It's not yours to maintain control of the infinite. Surrender."

The Breaking Point

When he said it, his words slammed into me, like a wave, as I stopped fighting. I gave the water to take me, not like I gave up control — but that I gave up the need to have control. My body began to soften, my breath deepened and I started to flow with the current rather than against it.

It then occurred a feeling that was beyond comprehension. The cold wasn't cold anymore, the river wasn't the river anymore. I could sense a connection so expansive, so pervasive that it shattered every border that I had ever known of. All that was water, stars, even the earth under my feet, alive, interrelated, infinite.

Not because I was hit with pain or fear, but because of the sense of awe that streamed down my face in tears. This was it. This was what Rudra had been bringing me to: A way of being of pure being, no self, just something greater, finite being an infinite.

I stepped out of the river; my body shook but my heart was still. He was quiet with pride when he handed me a blanket. He said simply, "You have tasted it." "This is now the real journey."

The night was different, more alive and we walked back to the cave. It was so clear the air, like, something had been unfurled about perception. I was lighter: not because I did something, but because I stopped doing something: wanting to do something.

I could feel the monks, waiting for us in the cave, anchoring me in the realness of all that was occurring. Sitting by fire, the warmth found its way to my bones, and I meditated on what had just happened.

It was never the infinite to be reached or found, but already waiting to be noticed. That wasn't giving up, it was opening up, it was allowing myself to be integrated into the flow, not trying to control it.

A soft crackling fire, I closed my eyes, inhaled deeply, and allowed the current within me to align with the current of the Universe. So, in that stillness, I knew that the journey was just starting, it was not over.

The Symphony of Wisdom

A golden hue shone from the cool stone walls of the cave as the fire flickered softly. The silence was solid; burdened with meaningfulness, not emptiness. Sitting cross-legged, damp from the river's embrace I felt fragile and powerful. Rudra sat, unwavering, his focus fixed while his presence pulled and refused to let me go. Each of the six monks that surrounded us had a quiet authority about them and an aura that was sacred knowledge.

I had no words. It had been still all this time picking up pieces of what I've gone through in the Ganga—the fear, the surrender, the infinity. Yet the night seemed far from over with its lessons.

Rudra's resonant and low voice broke through the silence. "Tonight, you will feel the fragments of wisdom as they flow through you. You will be guided into the essence of each individual monk, but to take them fully, you must flow all seven of them and see what can be glimpsed when you do."

Stability: The Unshakable Ground

The First Monk moved — deliberate movements, grounded posture. She took a single stone into his palm and held it up; smooth and calm on its surface, he put it in front of me.

Rudra said it reverently, "Sthiratva. The wisdom of stability."

The monk crouched, signaling for me to grab the stone. Its weight felt heavier than it looked but somehow that weight anchored me to an odd unfamiliar place.

Rudra instructed, "Feel the weight. The earth from under your feet, the roots of the greatest tree, the source of your core."

The monk pressed a stone against my chest and I followed her guidance. I felt its steadiness, its permanence, then. The thoughts started to slow in my mind, everything grounding itself again.

"The word 'stability' means not being static," Rudra said. "Stillness can be a lot more than just quiet; it is finding strength in stillness; it is standing firm even when the winds of change blow around you."

Compassion: The Warmth of the Heart

A second monk stood forward, holding a bowl of water that glinted with firelight in its surface. Her presence was serene warmth, she bowed head as she knelt before me, dipping the bowl and letting the water flow over my hands.

"Karuna," Rudra said softly. "The wisdom of compassion."

The monk had my hands in her hands and made me put the water gently back into the bowl. It was a simple act, that reached down something deep inside me, memories of moments in my life where kindness had made bridges, healed wounds, and helped me form connections.

"Compassion is the bridge that joins the heart with that of the mind," Rudra said. It teaches us to see others in ourselves, to love, not in obligation." We are all human. We belong to the flow of compassion."

The smile of the monk was small, gentle — and held the weight of lifetimes.

Discernment: Seeing Through the Veil

The eyes of the third monk were such that it was as if he could see through layer after layer of my being. Holding a single candle in his hands its flame didn't waver despite the cold cave air. He placed it in front of me, and gestured for me to watch the flame.

"Viveka," Rudra intoned. "The wisdom of discernment."

The monk leaned in close as I tried to stare into the flickering light. His voice a low murmur, "What do you see?" he asked.

"A flame," I replied.

"Look deeper," he said.

I let flame capture my attention. First, I saw only the shape of its dance. I stared longer at it, and saw its essence, its devouring of the wick, its lighting and its darkness.

"Discernment is the ability to see beyond appearances," Rudra said. "Perception of truth even when wrapped in illusion; clarity to see it. The wisdom is the ability to differentiate between the eternal and the temporal."

Courage: The Fire Within

The fourth monk stood up; his presence was commanding but it was also calm. With him he carried a small metal dish with a glowing ember, it was so hot in the dish that I could feel it from 5 feet away.

Rudra said his voice steady, "Sahas. The wisdom of courage."

The ember was held close to a monk who knelt before me. "Feel its warmth," he said. "It's your internal fire, your internal match to act, to take a step off the cliff into the unknown, into your fears."

I reached my hand out carefully, the warmth tickling my skin. Its glow was hypnotic and equally luring and awe-inspiring.

Rudra spoke in a firm, but still kind, tone, "Courage is not the absence of fear. But it is the decision to continue with it, despite it. As a way to carry the fire in you, and not as something that eats away, but instead as something that illuminates."

Introspection: Turning Inward

The fifth monk walked forward, her demeanor at rest and calm. In her hand was a polished mirror, spotless, which she set in my lap.

Rudra said slowly, "Antarmukha. Insight into introspection."

The monk motioned at me, to look in the mirror. I looked into my reflection and I saw beyond my face, the hard eyes and the tired features, the doubt and the strength and the hope that had taken me this far.

"Introspection is the courage to turn in", Rudra said. "To face your light, but also to face your shadows. This is the wisdom to know that the answers you seek aren't outside of you."

Looking my reflection in the mirror, feeling as though the journey wasn't about becoming something more but discovering what was there all the time.

Creation: Manifesting the Flow

While Vyom came nigh, he poured with bright energy, of seemingly without end, the ample charge full of potential and the infinite continuum of creation through merely thought and deed. He had a handful of seeds and he put them gently into my open palm.

Rudra said his voice with reverence "Srishti. The wisdom of creation."

The monk gestured me to put the seeds in soil close to the fire. He handed me a flask of water and I poured it over the seeds as directed.

"Making isn't just about creation," Rudra said. "It's about intention and action being in agreement and supporting the nurturing of your potential to grow. Being the alchemy of thought into reality."

I saw the water settle in the soil taking the seeds with it. It was sacred, a reminder that something else was happening in the same exact moment all around the world, that no one was making creation—that it was all a collaboration with the same energy flow of life.

Surrender: Becoming the Flow

Finally, Rudra stood; his presence was commanding, yet serene. His eyes stayed on mine as he stepped into the circle.

He said something in his soft yet resonant voice: "Samarpana. The wisdom to surrender."

He held out his hand motioning me to stand. Taking me to edge of the cave which opened onto the Ganga, where the sound of the Ganga could be heard roaring in the distance.

"Surrender is not about giving up. It's trusting the flow of life itself. It is the triumph point of Adira's stability, Ishani's compassion, Kapeesh's discernment, Sarthak's courage, Varya's introspection and Vyom's creation . If they don't surrender, then the fragments remain separate; if they do surrender, then they form a unitary whole which is taken over by the infinite." According to him, it's about living in sync with the infinite flow... 'becoming one with it."

Their truth was undeniable and the words sank deep into my soul. Then I closed my eyes to fall asleep to the rhythm of the river, the stillness of the earth, the fire within, and the breath that underlies it all.

"Surrender", said Rudra, "is the 'fulfillment' of all wisdom. The thread that places them together in wholeness."

The Circle Completes

The monks chant rose, so loud I could feel the energy in each and every cell of my being and also in each and every particle present in the cave. Each of those voices held a part of the wisdom they carried, in chunks of grounded stability, warm compassion, sharp discernment, fiery courage, reflective introspection, and vibrant creation. Thrown together, their voices weaved a fabric with those sound, echoing the seemingly infinite flow Rudra had described.

The echo of Ganga with the chant, it was as if the very sound of the Ganga was harmonizing to the chant, a natural symphony beyond my understanding, as I stood at the edge of the cave. Rudra faced me, his face serene, and calm.

With a signal, he invited me to reenter the circle.

I felt I was not walking but my legs were carrying me. I wasn't walking fast; it was slow and purposeful. At that moment I was feeling my legs were only utilizing the energy required to get me from point A to point B.

He said this circle is about wholeness. 'Each fragment of wisdom is not only around you, but also within you. Through this journey of surrender, we do not look for each fragment of our self as that which is external to us, but in awakening them within us."

I was not being judged by their monastic eyes, there was only an expectation, gentle; profound.

"Close your eyes," Rudra said.

Rudra started to guide me through a meditation, his voice soft, steady… As I closed my eyes.

He said, "Feel the earth beneath you. You've got the stability to hold you. This is not just the ground. This is your foundation; this is your strength."

Warmth ran up my body, footsteps upwards. It wasn't just physical, rather it was a grounding, a link to something solid, immovable.

"Now," Rudra continued, "feel your heart. Your compassion, that flows through you, that connects you to the world around."

Love, empathy, and connection suddenly surged in me. It was incredible, natural as if it was always there to be recognized.

Rudra Said, "Don't worry, , just focus on your mind. To see the truth beyond illusion is discernment."

Then the chaotic noise of my thoughts began to quiet, passing into a clarity that felt like a man seeing the light of dawn for the very first time.

He continued: "Feel the fire within. The fear that is in you but still takes you forward."

The energy growing in my chest felt both comforting, humbling and empowering.

"Keep turning inward," Rudra said. "The mirror of the soul and the gateway into yourself is introspection."

And in this stillness, I didn't know there was this depth within me, a well that could be drawn from for an endless supply of life. It wasn't a matter of just gazing inward— it was a matter of accepting who I found in there.

Rudra continued, "Now, feel the energy of creation. The ability to make the leap from intention into actuality, to see your own manifestation of your truth."

I felt a sense of possibility flood through me; a reminder that I was not just a passive observer, but a co-creator.

"Finally," almost a whisper Rudra said, "let it all go. Let the flow, the infinite take you over. Be certain that you are not apart from it—be it."

His words sunk in with me, the boundaries of my body evaporating. What had been fragments of wisdom weren't just lessons, they were parts of me, made alive and awake. It was for the first time that I felt whole not as an individual but as part of something much bigger.

I opened my eyes and the monks were still sitting around me, all serene. The embers of the fire were glowing softly because the fire had burned low.

His tone was both gentle, yet firm. "Begin truly living the infinite. This journey is not over, it's not over until every breath, every moment, every choice. The whole you what have awakened are not separate fragments. They lead you there to the infinite within."

The monks nodded in unison, not with exuberance, but with quiet approval that seemed to fill me with quiet confidence.

"You are ready," Rudra said. "You're not reaching a destination; you are simply embracing the flow. You live as the infinite as soon as you surrender."

The Infinite Journey

On the light of dawn breaking for the mountains just now, the circle was dissolved. Rudra stepped away, his presence both grounding and ethereal, as the monks returned to their silent meditations.

I went to the edge of the cave where from a distance the Ganga roared. The river was no longer something to be feared, just a force of nature, it was a reflection of the world that I had learned, all my experiences, all that I was becoming.

It was not over the journey, but for the first time, I did not want an endpoint. The infinite had not been something to find or something to achieve: it was something to live; something to be.

In that realization, I found a peace that words could never fully convey. The greatest truths aren't always expressed; they're simply thought in the restful breaks when we allow ourselves to be the flow.

Reflection for the Readers

Right now, take a moment and breathe, truly breathe. Breathe in, breathe out completely. Can you feel it? The rhythm of your breath, the still hum of your body, the energy powering that. That is your flow. You've had it with you all the time, you just needed to notice it.

What if we frame what the monks shared as lessons? What could you use more stability in, a solid, unshakable foundation to weather life's storms in your life? Where could you practice compassion even towards yourself? Where might you sharpen your ability to see through the illusion to the truth?

Celebrate which fears are you ready to face with courage. What would you turn inward to and why would you embrace introspection? How would you align with the power of creation in order to manifest what dream or intention? Last, what could you surrender control to and trust the flow of life?

These aren't Platonic notions meant only for mountaintop sages. These energies are available to each one of us in the very, everyday moments of our lives. If we allow it, staring water, planting seeds, or pausing to breathe deeply all carry the exact same profound wisdom.

Rudra, the river, and the mountains aren't separate from you. They are looking at the infinite potential within yourself and are mirrors. Your trip will look different, but the thread is the same. Most people try to reach this infinite, it's about remembering this was always here.

So, as you close this chapter, I invite you to pause and reflect: Where are you on your journey? What wisdom is trying to jump out of fragments to awaken you? The experiences I would have if I let go, surrendered, and embraced simplicity.

They don't live out there. Waiting for you to listen, they're in you. And it's not until you do that that you discover that the infinite is a state of being, not a destination. A flow you've been involved in the whole time.

CHAPTER 11

THE RIVER WITHIN

The River's Dual Nature

The river Ganga was relentless — its rhythm unbroken as it cut its way through the mountains. I stood by its banks hearing the hum of its flow through my chest. It wasn't water. It was life itself, bound for purpose and surrender, tracing paths out of nothing and avoiding obstacles without question.

I knelt, dunked my hands into the icy waters, and let its raw energy pour into each and every pore of my body. The river appeared as if it brought forth not just water, but stories of beginnings and endings, of stubborn resilience, of surrendering, of life and of death. And, for the first time, I wondered: Was the river reflecting the flow I had forgotten to exist inside of me, or was it educating me, or teaching me to flow?

I braced myself and turned to Rudra, who stood very still — a few steps away, staring at the water. "What is it about a river that causes it to seem vivacious?" My voice was barely audible above the roar of the current, I asked.

Rudra looked at me, a smile lighting up his face. He didn't explain this, just said "Because it's alive. The river is almost not water but movement, life, rhythm. That too, is a mirror of existence itself."

As I watched the Ganga, words lingered from his mouth. The waves crashed and tumbled over one another, the surface seeming at first chaotic. But below, the current didn't waver at all, not even at all those surging rapids above. Then I knew the river wasn't just a river, it was a lesson; a lesson about how to live.

Rudra continued, as if he'd been reading my thoughts, "In life, you're going to hit the surface: chaos, resistance, unpredictability. There is a current, though—the ever-moving infinite. You don't have to live fully, you can live accepted, you can play it safe, you don't have to rock the boat, but to live fully is to connect to that current, regardless of what's happening on the surface."

Reflection for the readers

We often face a choice between playing it safe and living fully. Take a moment to reflect on a time when you chose to play it safe:

- *What was the situation, and what held you back from taking a risk?*

- *What was the short-term benefit of playing it safe?*

- *What was the long-term cost of staying in your comfort zone?*

- *How did playing it safe affect your relationships, personal growth, and overall sense of fulfillment?*

> *- What would you do differently if faced with a similar choice today?*
>
> *Take a few moments to journal or meditate on these questions. Allow yourself to explore the complexities of your choices and the trade-offs you've made. What insights arise, and how might they inform your decisions moving forward?*

I allowed his words to hook inside of me as I continued to stare across the river and traced its path. It wasn't fighting; it just went up, adjusting to the rocks and cliffs and land in its way. And yet, it never stopped. It didn't falter. It did not ask about its journey. It just flowed.

The Power of Adaptation

It was a boulder jutting out from the middle of the river, stirring up swirling eddies in the water, Rudra gestured toward it. "Look at that rock," he said. Later Rudra's words echoed with Adira's lesson about stability. "Resistance was not stability, but rather being able to get your feet in the water while drifting through life's hurdles. The rock doesn't resist the river; it moves around it, over it, even through it. It's not a problem for the river. It is part of its path."

I felt that his words were so simple. How many times have I seen challenges in my life as immovable boulders and barriers to getting where I want to go? Yet the river had nothing of the sort to teach, and yet the river was teaching me that obstacles weren't barriers, but obstacles were part of the flow.

"Avoiding obstacles was not the point", Rudra said. "it's about recognizing them for who they really are in the things that they contributed to your journey. The river doesn't expend its energy fighting the rock and using its flow around it."

I closed my eyes and I thought to myself, what are my rocks in life, my doubts, my fears, my false losses? What if I didn't deny them, but allowed them to be a part of the journey with me? How would I let them mold me, as the river worked its way through the mountains?

When I stood watching the water, something changed in me. I had spent so much time fighting, fighting to control things, fighting against changes, fighting to prove myself to the world. The river was showing me another way, but... Fighting wasn't what it was about. Flowing and believing in the current even when it's not clear.

Rudra said, softly. 'The river flows because it knows its purpose. It doesn't wonder where it is going or why, it just flows. That's its nature. And that's your nature, too."

The weight of his words sunk in and I turned to him. "But what if I don't know what my purpose is?" my voice low and trailing off in uncertainty.

Rudra's gaze softened. "Your purpose is not something which you find but something which you become. So, just like the river, your purpose is to flow and live totally in each moment. With time the rest will reveal itself."

They were comforting, and they were challenging all at once. They asked me to stop wanting certainty; stop believing I knew how this would happen, trusting in a process I didn't completely understand. However, as I turned to look at the river, I knew that I could feel its power, I knew I didn't need to understand it to sense its wisdom. I just needed to be present.

The wind began to pick up, bringing with it the smell of wet earth, and the slightest smell of flowers from somewhere up the river. The river was speaking, I could feel the sensations, not with words; it was inviting me to listen.

I knelt down again, twiddling my fingers through the water. It sent a chill up my spine but I didn't pull away. I closed my eyes and let myself be guided by the rhythm of the river instead. It all ran together—the sound of the current, feel of the water, pull of the flow—into something else, into something greater, into the infinite.

"Do you feel it?" His voice was low but insistent, and Rudra asked.

I nodded because I just didn't know what to say about what was happening. I wasn't just feeling the river, it was feeling the flow in me, the connection between my breath, my body and the body of the world. I felt for the first time, that I was part of something greater than myself, more harmonic.

A Call to Trust

When the sun started setting behind the mountains and the valley was painted gold and amber, Rudra placed a hand on my shoulder. He said 'The river teaches us that it's alright to trust. Trusting the flow, trusting ourselves, and trusting life itself. That trust is what'll push you on—not just here, but ever and ever."

The weight of his words squeezed my chest and I looked up at him. Trust. The idea was so simple, but it had been the hardest lesson of all. How do you trust the unknown? How do you surrender to the current and let go of control?

Rudra's words were tinged with Ishani's quiet compassion. Rudra said, as if reading my mind, "The river doesn't ask those questions. It just flows. And so will you."

When we turned back to the riverbank to leave, I felt calm, a calm I hadn't felt in years. The Ganga had peeked into what it was like living in the flow, flowing with the current, with all the chaos and all the beauty of life. I didn't know all the answers, but I was ready to step up.

The purpose of the journey was not to the end; the journey was the flow. At that moment I knew I had already started.

The Dance of Resilience

The Ganga River was not an ordinary river. This was its one presence, magnetic, making me want to stay on its banks as if this place held answers to questions I hadn't yet dared to ask. The water, fierce and gentle, moved its force ever so slightly like it was whispering in the ancient truths that are silt and stories downstream. The ripples really seemed to be alive, it was as if the river was not just a metaphor for flow, but perhaps a teacher of resilience.

I strode along the bank, a feeling of reality provided by the soft crunch of pebbles underfoot. Rudra walked beside me, staying silent, and made me emote upon the view we saw. Currents of the river writhing together wove a symphony of activity. One current marched forward unyielding, and another spun in quiet corners, slow and deliberate.

"Do you see the dance?" The nagging sound of rushing water stopped as Rudra finally spoke.

I had stopped walking and turned to him. "The dance?" I was unsure of what he meant, I echoed.

He nodded toward the river. "Look closely. There is no single stream of the water: it is a union between the countless currents, each a soloist but still united with the whole. It's not one thing; it's a bunch of forces in harmony with one another."

I tried to see the river like Rudra, and watched more intently. And then it struck me: It wasn't as though the river's flow was uniform. It was a collaboration. It moved in some places fast, it lay asleep in some calm pools, and it rushed in others as if it had still a mind to decide which way to turn. But united, all these disparate movements formed something whole, something coherent and powerful.

"Perfection isn't what this is about," Rudra continued. "It's about harmony. It lets every current in the river find its place, knowing that a collection of drops is brought together in flowing and that every current gets there unto the ocean."

The Weight of Resistance

Rudra picks up a small rock and holds it out to me, as we start walking. He said, "Feel the weight of this."

The rock was so cool in my palm that I took it. Solid presence and was heavier than I expected.

"Well, this is resistance," said Rudra. "The weight you feel when you try to resist the current of life."

The river, he gestured to, was tumbling over bigger rocks, frothy cascades. "See what happens when water collides with a rock? Does it stop? Does it fight?"

"No," I said slowly. "It flows around it."

"Exactly," Rudra said, firmly. "The river doesn't stop flowing because of resistance — it gets shaped by it. The rock is accepted by the water, it is adapted to and moved on. If the rock is not the river's obstacle, it becomes part of the river's journey."

Turning the rock over in my hand, its rough edges scratched into my skin. How much of a load had I carried in my life? How many times had I stood against the change, hanging on to control, battling the inevitable? What if instead of fighting it, I learned how to just flow around it?

The Lesson of the Pebbles

The river got shallow and spread out into a clear, calm section, showing the smooth pebbles where its bottom now lay. Rudra crouched, collected a handful of the small stones, and let them fall through his fingers back into the water.

He held up one between his thumb and forefinger and asked, "Do you see these pebbles? They were once sharp, jagged and rough…each one. The river has worn them down over time, polishing away the topmost edges with every current passing over them."

I knelt down beside him, hovering my hand over the water to gather up a pebble. Its surface shone in the sun, but it was smooth and cool. "How does the river do it?" I looked at the transformation and asked.

Rudra's words belonged to their wisdom of creation, brought to life by Vyom. Rudra said, "Through persistence. The river doesn't rush. It doesn't make the stones change. It is nothing more than it being worn down over time, wearing away the rough edges. That is the power of resilience — not fighting, but continuing."

I brought my attention over to the pebble in my hand, its simplicity concealing its travel. It wasn't pebble, it was a testimony of the river's patience and determination. In that moment, I watched myself in the stone. My rough edges didn't need to be smoothed out, my jagged doubts and fears didn't need to be overcome — they were me, and could be softened, shaped, and polished in the flow of life.

Rudra got up saying, "The river isn't in a hurry. It trusts the process. And so should you."

Becoming Part of the Flow

The sun crested to new heights as the river shone with new intensity of shimmer, the surface reflecting like a mirror. Rudra stopped and turned to me, and he looked serious. The river had become recognizable to you from the outside, he said. "It's time to feel it from within."

I didn't know what he meant, so I frowned. "What do you mean?"

The current had powered up and Rudra pointed to a section of the river. "Get in the water," he told me. "Feel the flow for yourself."

But I couldn't argue with the thought of stepping into icy water, made shiver go up my spine. I took off my shoes, rolled up my pants and waded cautiously into the river. I was shocked at the cold—first—I felt jolted through my body and then acclimated, letting the current wrap my legs.

Rudra called from the bank, "Close your eyes. Stop resisting the current. Let it move you."

I closed my eyes, stood still, and started feeling the water pushing against me. It wasn't a physical sensation: it was an invitation. The current wasn't trying to knock me down, it was asking me to trust the flow, to let go of my footing and let it carry me.

For a moment, I hesitated. The ground under my feet was solid and safe. However, Rudra's words rang true in my mind, I knew safety wasn't what I wanted. I needed to flow.

I took a deep breath and lifted one foot off the ground then the next. There was the current, it grabbed me immediately and took me down the river. This panic started flailing against the water; Sarthak's courage made Rudra's command. "Surrender!" Through all of the chaos, Rudra's voice cut through.

And so, I did. So, I simply stopped fighting, and I let the river take me. That moment was the moment something shifted within me. What wasn't my enemy was the current—it was my guide. I wouldn't die from it rather it would teach me how to live.

The Harmony of Nature

Dripping and breathless, I found myself eventually coming out of that river, and I had a strange sense of peace. The chaos of the current was forgotten, replaced by a stillness in me so profound, that I felt as though the river had washed away not just the dirt from my skin, but the resistance of my soul.

Knowing, Rudra handed me a dry cloth. Rudra spoke with Kapeesh's wisdom of discernment. He said, "The river is a mirror", as I dried myself off. "It brings to you what you need to see, whether you're ready for it or not," he said.

I nodded, unable to form the words. In a single moment, the river had shown me more than what I had learned in years of searching. It had taught me how resilient I was, how beautiful surrender was, and how infinite potential I have, all I had to do is trust the flow within.

The Ganga roared behind us as we walked back to the cave, roaring both fiercely and gently. Then I realized that the river was not just a metaphor, but a teacher, a guide, and a representation of the infinite.

I wasn't done with the journey, but for the first time, I felt ready to tackle it. Because the river had shown me the truth: You don't control the current in life, you become part of it.

Something was different about the return to the cave after I had been immersed in the river. I was light in body though drenched, and cold. It wasn't purely the physical release of tension, but there was something about the river washing parts of me that I didn't even know needed to be washed off. My mind seemed clearer: no longer cluttered with all those thoughts. The river had spoken and its words still echoed through me.

The Whisper of the Infinite

The familiar stillness of the cave greeted me back. My skin soaked in the heat of the fire in the center crackled softly. I sat cross-legged among the monks. His presence was commanding without being unseemly; Rudra remained standing. For the first time, he appeared to look at me and I felt I actually saw him, not as a guide or as a monk, but in a reflection of the journey that I was on.

Rudra said, his voice resonant, low: "The river has begun its work. The lessons don't end when the water of the river merges with the ocean. The living metaphor is that the river is like life, always flowing, constantly moving, always teaching."

He stopped, letting his words spread across the stream bed the way pebbles sunk into the bottom. The silence that descended wasn't empty; it was filled with the potential that you find in the calm before a great truth is revealed.

"What did you feel when you let the current take you?" he continued.

The water had hit me with a mass of emotions and I thought for a moment. "At first, fear," I admitted. "Fear of the way I lose myself. But then... freedom. "Then, I stopped fighting and I was free."

Rudra nodded, his face easing. "That is the essence of the river's lesson: to let go. Giving up with control is not defeat. The flow does not want to defeat you; it wants to guide you. The river brings you; it doesn't drown you. It gets you to where you are meant to be."

The Symphony of Connection

With A small bowl of water one of the monks stepped forward towards me. He set it in front of me and motioned for me to check it out. This surface was still; pristine to reflect my reflection.

Rudra pointed to the reflection, "This is you. One drop, and it is one of a kind. But when a drop enters the river, what happens then?"

Off the cuff, I answered, "It becomes part of the whole."

"Exactly," Rudra said. Still, the drop doesn't disappear. It doesn't lose its essence; it just became part of something bigger. This is all on connection. You do not stand apart from the world in which you live. "You are the drop, and just as much you are the river."

I felt a lump in my throat as he spoke. The words hit something inside me beyond my conscious thought. The isolation overwhelmed so much of my life; I had spent so much of my life wondering how to define myself in a world that could seem so big at times. As I sat here with the monks though I started to notice the threads that linked everything together—the river, the mountains, the monks, and myself.

The monks started chanting one by one. Their voices were soft-spoken and musical, complementing one another with a harmony that coursed over the very air. The sound wasn't only music, no. It was a call to mind what Rudra said, of the oneness of all things, a symphony tapestry of voices sounding together to make something more than the individual parts.

The Flow Within

The chant fell away, and Rudra gestured me to close my eyes. The voice that was of Varya seemed to guide me. "Now, turn inward," she said. "Feel the flow within you."

I obeyed and turned my focus to my breath. Inhale, exhale. Inhale, exhale. With every cycle, I became more aware of the energy that was flowing through my body. It was almost subtle at first, a gentle current that started deep inside of me and spread out. Yet, the more I went on the stronger, the more vivid it became, so strong that it felt like I was the river.

" Be one with the river, its flow is your essence, its ripples are your thoughts. " Rudra spoke, stitching my voice back together through his own, like the current of the Ganga. "It's the string that holds you to the movement of energy. Come back to it when you feel lost. True faith will tell you that when you feel overwhelmed it is speaking. It will carry you."

His words were simple and I caught it. How many times had I forgotten to take a breath, considering it was just background biological activity? I realized now, it was so much more. The bridge—where physical and spiritual, and the finite and infinite, meets.

I felt immanently harmonious as I sat there, listening to the rhythm of my breath. It wasn't something outside of me, it was in me, just as much a part of me as the blood in my veins or the thoughts in my mind.

Returning to the River

The fire had gone lower, its embers flickering in this dim light when I opened my eyes. While the monks stayed in place, they really grounded the space. Rudra stood up and gestured for me to come with him.

The cool night air wrapped around us like a blanket; we stepped outside. The river roared away in the distance a fierce sound soothing. Looking low in the sky, the moon glared down at us in its silvery light.

He led me to the riverbank and the water sparkled liquid light. Standing beside me his eyes were locked on the current.

"Do you see it now?" he whispered inaudibly.

I nodded, the river tracing its path through the valley, caught in my eyes. "It's not water," I said. "It's life. Movement. Connection."

Rudra smiled a rare combination of love and pride on his face. He said: "The river is a teacher. Though the lessons of its confinement are for the water, they are not just for the water. For all of us, they are. To live is to flow. To resist is to suffer. To live truly, though, is to surrender—to submit to what is, to trust what's happening in the moment."

The river roared in the silence between us and I felt such a deep feeling of gratitude. I appreciate the journey, the hardship, and the object lessons that have brought me to where I am now. Not just had the river let me see the power of surrender, but also the beauty of resilience.

He said finally, "Life is not going to be so easy" and stopped talking. "You will have rocks in your path that threaten to pull you under. But remember this: it's one of those things that the river always finds its way. It doesn't stop. It doesn't give up. It flows, no matter what."

The truth of his words sank in, and I nodded. The river was a metaphor, but also a guide, a reminder to me that in the face of obstacles I could keep moving. I could keep flowing.

Reflection for the Journey Ahead: I put down my head that night, letting the cool stone with which I now lay and the sound of the river that echoed in the distance draws me towards tranquility. Far from over, the journey wasn't. For the first time, for once I was ready to face whatever was coming at me.

The river said to me that even reaching a destination doesn't constitute life. That's the flow—the moments of connection, lessons of practicing resilience, and what it means to surrender elegance. In that flow, I discovered how to know not only answers but to know what it is to live.

I wasn't only outside the river, but I was inside it, too. Closing my eyes, I knew I would continue to carry the lessons from this journey forward; moving ever forward, ever resilient, ever connected.

Reflection for the Readers

Have you ever watched a river and felt its pull, not just the physical current of a river, but the heart of the river? There are things the river tells us that we can't quite put into words. It is beautiful in movement, inevitable change, and resilient strength. As you reflect on this chapter, consider these questions:

What are the rocks in your path? The rocks in your path. What in your life feels immovable right now? The river reminds us that, even if she's the biggest boulder of all, she will still wear down if only she persists long enough.

Are you resisting the flow? Where are you tight in your life, too tight, too controlling, too afraid, too critical, too anything? The river's lesson is simple yet profound: letting go doesn't mean losing control, it means trusting the journey.

How do you maintain a connection to the flow within? The river is constant, grounding, life-sustaining, just like it is. So is your breath. Take a moment to focus on it. Inhale deeply. Exhale fully. Let the rhythm, the flow, the life feel for you.

The river within us is the one who can guide us and reflect us. It's like the preaching of Adira, Ishani, Varya, Kapeesh, Sarthak, and Vyom that talk of our fears, our strengths, and how well we can adapt and grow. Its current whispers a truth that can transform how we navigate life's challenges: To flow is to trust and to live is to flow.

Be sure to remember the river's lesson as you keep going. The path isn't to end up somewhere but to bask in the experience. Let the river teach you, and teach you from its resilience. What else is there to say, you can't see the other side but that never stops the river in its path. So can you.

CHAPTER 12

RETURNING HOME

The Silent Farewell

Golden rays of light filtered through the mouth of the cave and fell on the stone walls. It burned itself to embers at the center, its warmth was fading, but not yet gone. This time the silence in the cave wasn't empty or heavy, but it was full of unspoken understanding. The silence was the silence of endings and beginnings, of the impermanent.

Their presence was as calm and steady as ever, the monks were seated in their usual circle. Today the air held a weightiness to it, a sense that even the mountains knew this chapter of the journey was coming to a close.

In a cave, Rudra sat beside me, gazing at the horizon through its opening. Just the sun had started to appear and color the sky with shades of orange and pink. Neither of us spoke for a long moment. There were no words, it felt words were just unnecessary things that got in the way of that stillness.

After a moment, Rudra spoke . "You will be leaving soon,". His voice sounded strange to my ears — as if it were someone else's voice.

He looked at me; the expression on his face unreadable, but kind. He said: "Every journey has to come to an end. But it's not as final as it seems, endings. All they are is transitions to take you from one path to the next."

The lump in my throat meant I couldn't respond but I nodded anyway. How do you leave somewhere—even when you are reluctant to do so—when the people who have made you into your own person reside there? How do you let go of a part of yourself?

Packing the Intangible

Their silence reflected mine, and the monks had little to say. Moving with their usual grace they attended to the fire, fetched water, and morning meditation practice. Their mundane, ordinary actions took on sacred, holy qualities as if their constant weaving of invisible threads into the fibers of my final moments were none of that, but something more.

Varya, the keeper of introspection, gave me a small bundle of cloth-wrapped thing. I unfolded it to see a handful of smooth, polished stones—pebbles that the river had worn to its smooth shape.

"Take these," she said simply. "This a reminder that the flow is always with you."

So, whenever she spoke, it would reach me deep inside. The stones weren't just souvenirs, they were symbols of everything I had learned, the power of persistence, the beauty of surrender, beauty of resilience through adaptation.

The stones, how their weight was both grounding and comforting, I slipped them into my bag.

Hurrying up to the river, Rudra took hold of a small bowl of water and came to me. He said it softly, but firmly. "Drink."

Taking one bowel to my lips, I paused for a moment. The water was crisp and cool to taste, the unmistakable taste of the Ganga. I felt the energy pulsing through me as if it were from the river itself stamping my name my existence the infinite river into my existence .

"Not just water," Rudra said, as I placed the empty bowl. "Life is, always, moving, and flow is the essence of it: a reminder. Your river sits in you now. It will guide you 'wherever you go.'"

The Final Teaching

After morning rituals, the monks gathered in a circle, staring at me with serene faces. Their presence was commanding, yet humble, and Rudra stood at the center.

"Not too far is one final teaching," he said at last when his voice was steady. "It is the simplest and yet the most profound: Life is fleeting. What moments you spend here, what you learn, and whom you connect with are all temporary. But that's the beauty. The meaning of everything is impermanence."

There was a wave of emotion that rose in me; Gratitude, sadness, and a quiet pragmatic acceptance. There was no question that his words had become truth. Life's brevity was not something to lament over, to regret, to mourn off either — it was something to acknowledge and cherish.

Rudra looked around the circle, continuing. "The only wisdom you have found here is not intended to be under lock and key in this place. It has to be in motion, like the river, out there to the world. What you have learned is not really understood until you have lived. And to live fully you have to allow it to flow."

His words filled my ears and cut me to the core of my being. I realized then that this journey wasn't ending; it was becoming. I needed to become something else. The path I had taken to get here was becoming the path I would take to leave there; the lessons carried would mold the steps taken.

The monks moved up one by one, giving small gestures: the bow of the head, the touch of the hand, quiet words. You could feel their blessings, unspoken but there, every promise that we would always be connected, even across the distance.

The last one to step forward was Rudra. His grip was firm, but gentle, as he placed a hand on my shoulder. "Remember," he said, so softly that you could hear the panic in his voice, "We are not leaving you behind. You are carrying us with you. But the seven fragments carry the wisdom of your infinite lives. Let it guide you, always."

A Moment of Stillness

I was facing the cave entrance, prepared to leave, standing and looking out at mountains and sky, and sky and mountains. The faint scent of pine and earth swept into me on the wind; this world could not keep the rest of my world from me.

Rudra joined me. We stood in silence for some time under the weight of the moment.

Finally, he asked if I was ready.

Taking a deep breath, I felt mountain air fill my lungs. I nodded, though my voice shook.

His gaze fell in line with the horizon and he nodded. He said "the path ahead 'will not be easy.' But you are ready. Trust the flow. Trust yourself, and trust life. Remember, the infinite is always within you."

The last step fell to me, he stepped back and said those words. I started the descent down the mountain as the cave became smaller behind me, sadness for leaving, gratitude for the journey, and quiet resolve to bring forward the lessons I had learned.

It was a river that roared in the distance; the current was an ongoing reminder that everything was connected. But I walked away and I realized I wasn't leaving anything behind. I stepped out into the world beyond and the cave, the monks, Rudra, they were all me now, all streaming through me.

Reflection for the Reader

Do you know those times when past and future are blended, the presence is both ephemeral and everlasting? As you reflect on this part of the journey, consider:

> *What in your life's sacred spaces have you carried?*
>
> *What is the process of integrating those lessons into the everyday flow of existence?*
>
> *How do you embrace the impermanence of life, creating meaning from it?*
>
> *The journey back home is not about leaving something behind, it is to carry it in yourselves, empowered by Adira, Ishani, Kapeesh, Sarthak, Varya, Vyom, and Rudra. Trust that every step, no matter how small, is part of the infinite flow, and let the lessons you've learned mold the path ahead.*

Walking the Path Forward

It was physically and emotionally devastating on the cold ride down the mountain. With every step away from the cave, my body felt like a step further from my world of mine, yet a world that was still calling me back. Now the gravel beneath my feet seemed to crunch louder, and the wind nipping around my fingers seemed colder as if the mountain itself said goodbye with a silent sigh.

Only once did I glance back, the cave's entrance, a dark maw swallowed now, a small mark against the vast rock face. Their silhouettes were briefly visible in the distance behind, serving as only Rudra and the monks. I only had the weight of their words and the imprint of their presence on my soul — no photograph, no physical keepsake, or memory of the time I spent here.

I stopped for an instant, holding the bundle of stones the monks had given me. Nothing in life is coincidence they were exactly 7 stones. They were each an energy source, bursting with the seven fragments of wisdom I now had, Adira's stability, Ishani's compassion, Kapeesh's discernment, Sarthak's courage, Varya's introspection, Vyom's creation, Rudra's surrender. Now it was no longer something that I needed to reach outside of myself for – it was a part of my being.

Down the narrow trail, I went, willing myself to forget every fifth or sixth step as the rhythm of my steps tallied with the river running below. Its roar was the constant companion, the voice that was always there, that always assured, always insistent, as if so gently, imploring me to trust whatever lay ahead of me.

The First Test of Patience

As I kept going down, the path became steeper, and the loose rocks were in danger of letting me slip off it. Yet my body, still weakly recovering from the cave's transformative rituals was aching. I took short breaths, and the ache in my legs told me about my physical limitations.

I caught a corner just in time at one particularly tricky section of the trail that I would have fallen on. I was threatened that frustration would undo the peace I had found. "Why is this so hard?" The words came out of my mouth, uttered while I kept muttering to myself before I could stop them.

And then I remembered Rudra's voice: "Never fight the rocks, flow around them."

I eyed my past, closing my eyes in order to control my breathing. The trail wasn't enemies, it was part of the journey. It was teaching me patience, resilience, each stone each uneasy step. A slow breath escaped my lips and my body relaxed, my mind was quieted and I resumed the descent.

And it wasn't about getting down as fast as you could but it's about being present with each step, being stable even when the ground isn't.

The world was sharper, louder, more vivid than it had been before, and when I finally reached the base of the mountain. The hum of life came back in small ways, the birds chirping, the leaves rustling, a sound of the far distant village market. The sounds were almost jarring, after the profound stillness of the caves, but they were also alive, a reminder that the rhythm of existence does not stop.

Its current was strong and it was swift and cut the valley. Its magnetic pull drew me towards its banks and I walked towards them. The river had taught me, reflected me, and led me. I had surrendered and shown resilience to it and as I stood by it again, I was grateful.

I knelt down and let my fingers trail there in the water. The icy chill made me shiver, but I didn't pull away. I closed my eyes, instead, and leaned into the rush of the current, the whisper of the wind, the quiet beating of my heart.

It was a river that was no longer just a metaphor, but a part of me, as was each breath and every thought. I stood there and felt a quiet resolve find a cranny and make a nest inside me.

Lessons I learned on this journey would not be left here, at the river's edge. They were supposed to ripple into the world beyond and hit every part of my life.

But the 'Weight of the World Returns.'

Feeling a bit surreal, I was back in Rishikesh. It was nothing like the mountains, which were silent and empty except for the crisp air — it was the densely packed streets, the chatter of the people, and the smell of incense and street food. The events of life here rushed forward with a chaotic swirled purposefulness.

I drifted from the wide, open world to the narrow lanes, detaching myself from here, like I was from a distance observing. It wasn't an unpleasant feeling, but, as if I had found some stillness in the mountains, a buffer from the world, that allowed me to engage with it without being overwhelmed by it all.

And again, I found myself at the banks of the Ganga, surrounded by people (pilgrims, tourists, locals). They all had their own story, their own struggles and triumphs as well. I watched them and realized that the river wasn't just my teacher, but everybody's. Its lessons were universal and crossed the air freely for anyone willing to hear.

Final Conversation with Rudra

It was crisp, sharp, mountain air, the sun low on the horizon and staining the sky golden, burnished amber. I stood at the edge of the plateau, silhouetted against the expansive valley below. From a distance, I thought I saw Rudra and rushed towards him. He turned as I approached, his face was relaxed, but there was a definite weight of purpose to him. He had followed me without me being aware, the complete path down the mountain and this final visit was the culmination of everything.

My heart was so heavy with the separation to come but lighter with clarity. There was this oppressive silence between us, the kind that says just enough without having to say anything at all. His voice quiet, yet resolute, Rudra finally broke it.

"So, you say, Cherag," as he looked with solemn intent towards the horizon. "It's not easier down this path; it's just different. When you return to the world, the world will not meet you with the stillness of these mountains, or the wisdom of the monks. You'll be tested in ways you can't even begin to conceive of right now."

His words felt like a blanket of truth, consuming over me. There was a moment I wanted to reply, but the weight of the moment kept my mouth shut. He turned around, however, to face me entirely, the piercing yet gentle eyes landing on me.

His tone became urgent as if he had to ask something. "Do you trust yourself?" It smacked me like a jolt. Trust myself? I hadn't really asked myself that. It took me a moment to know what to say.

"I… I think so," I said finally, except the words sounded empty, even to my own ears.

Rudra's gaze didn't waver. "Cherag, you've seen the river. You've felt its flow. You know its lessons. You have learned to surrender."

The Road Ahead

He stopped, letting the words penetrate, then continued. "It wasn't a coincidence that you were here. All the mountains, the monks, and the river were part of the universal plan. This was not a journey to understand, it was a journey to become."

I choked back a lump as his words weighed on my chest. "What do you mean?" I asked softly.

Rudra pointed to the valley. Next to it, the Ganga serpentine, a crushed sequin of silver in the dying of light. "The river doesn't know where it's going, it only knows it's the river. You flow too— not with force, not with resistance, but with surrender."

His voice dropped almost into a conspiratorial whisper and he stepped closer. "Adira's stability, Ishani's compassion, Kapeesh's discernment, Sarthak's courage, Varya's introspection, Vyom's creation, and my surrender make up the seven fragments of wisdom —they are not lessons to learn and leave behind. They are currents to live by. Stability grounds you. Compassion connects you. Discernment guides you. Courage moves you. Introspection centers you. Creation empowers you. And Surrender makes you infinite."

Each of his words rode me like the river itself, each one full of truth that struck down at me deep inside. My mind was asking me a dozen questions I wanted to ask him. "But what if I falter? What if I fail?"

The Test of Trust

Rudra smiled. He said, "You will falter. And you will fail. Failure is not the opposite of flow; it's part of it. The river tumbles over rocks, whirls its water, and even overflows its banks. But it never stops. It never doubts its journey."

Its weight grounding and reassuring he placed a hand on my shoulder. "The river doesn't flow because it is not perfect. It flows because it trusts. Trust the current, Cherag. What wisdom do you carry within you, trust it. Remember that the universe has put you exactly in the place you are supposed to be "

The fairness of it all paralyzed me, and made me feel tears well up at the corners of my eyes, they weren't from sadness, but a sense of being seen, being understood, and being trusted. This wasn't just advice he was giving me; it was a roadmap to instigate grace and resilience in a world otherwise dominated by chaos.

Rudra took a step backward, his eyes unflinching. "This is not the end of your journey Cherag. It is only the beginning. The Mountains aren't ones meant to hold you—they're meant to ready you. We've covered so much while working together and now you must bear what you've learned here into the world. Wisdom knows, wisdom lives it, and it doesn't live as an ideal. If you allow the seven fragments to guide you, not as seven pieces but as one flow. It will flow through you. Into the infinite being of energy, and its existence"

He pointed again to the Ganga. "The river does not resist. It moves, adapts, and flows. Be the flow, Cherag. Let that wisdom run through you and into their lives. That is your path. That is your purpose."

For a moment he wanted to forget the enormity of his words. A weight to carry the wisdom Then I remembered the river—how effortlessly it moved, without any obstacles, yet it didn't abandon the obstacles as part of its journey.

The final words in Rudra's voice had taken on a quiet confidence. "You are ready," he said. "You might not feel it today, but you will. The current will carry you. Surrender and let it flow".

The Farewell

He stretched out his hand as the sun set on the horizon. The gesture was simple and profound and I took it. In that handshake was an undertone of promise—an undertone of promise to honor his journey, his lessons, and his trust in me.

I said, breaking my voice a little. I felt it was inadequate, but that was all I could do.

Rudra nodded, not rushing, and he was serene. He said: 'The river inside you is already flowing.' "Now, go. The world is waiting." I knelt, touching his feet to seek his blessing. He placed his hand on my head, and as I rose, he enveloped me in a warm hug. It was a hug that still feels like a blanket woven from the majesty of the mountains, the serenity of the rivers, the blessings of the monks, and the trust we shared.

The journey had begun, not ended. I felt ready to flow.

The First Act of Integration

On my way out of Rishikesh, I went to an ashram facing the river. Quiet and unassuming, it was no place for the crowds. I went to a small meditation hall and sat cross-legged on the floor, my back straight and my hands lightly on my knees.

I shut my eyes and calmed my mind. Inhale, exhale. Inhale, exhale. A rhythmic continuity that I was tied to the current and flowed within.

I meditated and the noise of the world faded away in the background. The thoughts flooded back, power of the river, the monks' lessons, the thousand pictures of seven fragments, overwhelming me with the realization that none were separate from the other and none are separate from me.

I opened my eyes, no longer confused. This wasn't a journey about leaving the world behind; it was a journey about coming back to a world seen with the eyes of a newness, heart open to the chaos, and beauty of it all.

When I stood up to go, I turned one last time at the meditation hall. True, it wasn't the mountains or the cave; but it had its own stillness, a stillness to invite connection into the infinite.

> ### Reflection for the Reader
>
> *As you navigate your own path, consider:*
>
> *What do you do with the lessons of sacred spaces in the everyday stream of life?*
>
> *How do we work to integrate wisdom into moments of chaos and challenge?*
>
> *What is it like to wear life's brevity not as a restriction, but as a call to be fully engaged with true authenticity?*

Coming back home is about building a new one crafted around what you've learned. Simply trust the flow and let it set you on the next step.

CHAPTER 13

WALKING THE INNER JOURNEY

The Journey is Never Over

Quiet in the cab from the foothills to the Dehradun airport saved by the hum of the car's engine and the occasional light chattering from the driver, who wanted to tell stories about the mountains. I politely listened while my mind was elsewhere, decanting the moments of my time with the monks and Rudra. I watched the twists and turns of the winding road and my thoughts, each mile taking me further from the cave, and bringing me closer to the world I had been in before.

The air was crisp as we were descending down the mountain and it replaced with the warmth of the plains. The temperature change was so slight yet apparent, like when you concluded one part of a book and went on to the next. I rolled down the window and the breeze took away the stillness that I had known in the mountains but I realized that it wasn't an external thing anymore. It was within me now.

There was hardly anything else on that road, except the occasional roadside temple or tea stall breaking the monotony of the journey. From time to time, I would catch glimpses of the Ganga, its waters flowing steadily with the obvious impression of the lessons that it taught me. I craned my neck as the cab crossed a bridge to get one last look at the river. Its surface was deceptively chaotic, its current was unyielding; it shimmered under the afternoon sun.

Rudra's voice echoed in my mind; you carry the river now. It was a thought that comforted me but had the weight of responsibility to it. I wasn't just leaving the mountains; I was taking their essence out to the world beyond.

The Weight of Transition

I made my way through the check-in and the security screening, only to feel it all was strangely alien at the airport. The noise and bustle of travelers rushing towards their gates were almost overwhelming, after weeks of simplicity. I clung to smooth stones the monks had given me that now sat in my pocket.

Ishani's compassion, Kapeesh's discernment, Sarthak's courage, Varya's introspection, Vyom's creation, Rudra's surrender and Adira's stability: These weren't only concepts, they were things, the knowledge the monks had passed on to me and written inside me. I made my way through the terminal, realizing that the journey had less to do with going back to the life I had, than it did with living it anew. Along with figuring out the lessons, what I was really trying to do was integrate them, to let them ripple through my actions and my choices.

I headed over to the boarding gate, grabbed my corner of the room, found some peaceful space, and pulled out my journal.

The pages were full of mountain reflections, already, but I felt compelled to write again, sitting amongst the chaos of the airport.

The river taught me to flow, but I can't seem to flow when life feels stagnant.

The monks taught me how to surrender but what do I do with surrender in a world that needs to be in control?

I learned how to listen from the mountains and so how do I hear such stillness amidst such noise?

They came quickly on the questions, more elusive in their answers. As I wrote, I started to realize with some clarity. These lessons weren't about how to solve life's problems, they were about how to guide one through them. This wasn't a destination, a morality tale to be forgotten and lost to memory. This wisdom was a practice, a way of being, keep flowing through the fragments of wisdom and merge into the infinite.

The Flight Home

The flight to Mumbai was unaffecting. The plane climbed and I watched the mountains reduce until they were little more than blurs against the edge of the world. The quiet resolve that had been growing in me tempered the pang of longing in my heart, but the longing was there, and I felt it tugging at me.

The monks had been clear: Knowledge, once picked, wasn't supposed to be left in the mountains. It should have extended and spread like ripples through the outside world. The city life challenges were not barriers, they were opportunities to live out those lessons.

I reached into my bag, extracting the bundle of stones, as the plane leveled off. Their weight was soothing. Each one represented a fragment of the journey, a reminder of the truths I now carried:

Stability grounds you.
Compassion connects you.
Discernment guides you.
Courage moves you.
Introspection centers you.
Creation empowers you.
Surrender makes you infinite.

The stones were smooth in my palm as they rolled over my hand, cooling against my skin. They weren't just symbols, they were anchors to remind me of the flow of the river, the stillness of the cave, and the wisdom of the monks.

As the plane started its descent into Mumbai, city lights suddenly appeared a maze of brightness against the inky darkness of the sea. It was uncontained, it was beautiful, it was overwhelming, it was alive. Upon touchdown, I was a combination of both excited and nervous to see the magic of me coming back to life. I was returning to the city that was familiar but as someone else entirely.

The streets outside were full of life, with cars honking, traffic, vendors, and people weaving around. This, of course, was far from the quiet of the mountains, but it had its own rhythm and its own flow. I got in my cab and gave the driver my address and we started the trip home.

The river's lessons echoed in my mind: flow, adapt, trust. It wasn't about leaving one world for another; it was about discovering the current, the thread, a seemingly invisible thread weaving the sacred and the mundane into a single fabric.

The First Night Back

The cab pulled up in front of my house, the headlights sweeping across the familiar contours of the building I had left behind. It felt both unchanged and yet, in some way, completely new. My heart pounded in my chest, not from exhaustion, not from the weight of the journey, but from something else—something deeper, something I hadn't felt in a long time.

I took the elevator up to my apartment and rang the bell. The door opened and Sabah opened the door. For a split second, she just looked at me, her breath caught in her chest, her hands frozen, as if unsure whether this was real or just something she had imagined too many times in my absence. And then, before I could say anything, she hugged me. She didn't speak. Neither did I. Words would have ruined it. Her arms wrapped around me, holding me tight, as if to say, You're here. You're real. You came back. And I held her just the same.

A small gasp. Tiny footsteps.

"Dadda?"

I turned just as my boys, Arhum and Aarish, appeared in the doorway, their sleepy eyes widening in disbelief. For a moment, they just stared. Then, like a dam breaking, they bolted toward me.

"Daddaaaa!"

They crashed into me, their tiny arms gripping my legs, their faces pressing into me, as if making sure I was solid, making sure I wasn't just a dream. I knelt down, pulling them into me. My throat clenched. The weight of a month apart, of missing their voices, their giggles, their little hands reaching for mine—it all came rushing in at once.

"You came back!" Aarish whispered. "I missed you, Dadda," Arhum said, his grip tightening as if afraid I'd disappear again. I couldn't speak. I just held them. Held them with everything I had.

Sabah knelt beside us, her hand resting on my back, her eyes brimming with something between relief and quiet knowing. She had held it all together while I was gone. She had carried the weight of my absence, had answered their questions, had waited—patiently, lovingly.

I looked at her, then at my boys, and something inside me settled. I had climbed mountains, crossed rivers, surrendered to silence, and found myself in places I never thought to look. But this—this was the moment that made it all real. I was home.

And in their laughter, in their touch, in the way my boys refused to let go, in the way Sabah wiped tears from my cheek without saying a word—I knew I had never truly been lost. I had always been making my way back.

That night, long after the laughter had faded and the house had settled into silence, I found myself awake, standing near the window of our bedroom. The city stretched beyond me, alive as ever, the distant horns of late-night traffic, the occasional bark of a street dog, the flickering glow of lights in homes where life was still unfolding.

Mumbai had always been loud and restless. And yet, as I stood there, breathing in the familiar warmth of home, I realized something strange—the silence was still with me. I closed my eyes. The weight of the mountains was in my breath. The rhythm of the Ganga still pulsed in my chest. The echoes of Rudra's voice, of the monks' teachings, of the wind moving through the caves—it was all here, as much a part of me as the life I was stepping back into.

I wasn't the same man who had left. I had learned to listen—not just to the world, but to the spaces in between. To the stillness beneath the noise. And now, standing under the open sky, Rudra's last words rushed back. "The last lesson is not given here. It is waiting for you… out there." I finally understood what they meant. The real test wasn't in the mountains—it was here, in the world I had always known. In the demands of daily life, in the pull of old habits, in the chaos that would try to shake me.

Could I hold the silence in the noise? Could I carry the stillness with me? I inhaled deeply, filling my lungs with the night air. Yes. I could. Because the journey wasn't over. It had just begun.

The Ripples Begin

These first few days back were surreal. Making tea, reading emails, or walking through crowded streets felt foreign. It was as if I was suddenly seeing the world with a new lens, and noticing details I had never noticed before. The rustle of leaves outside my window and the faint hum of the fan, the warmth of sunlight on my skin everything carried a weight, a significance I couldn't quite put into words.

However, as clarity descended, it became uncomfortable. The city lived at a relentless pace and it churned against the stillness I had fostered in the mountains. The noise of modern life drowned out the inner calm I had worked so hard to cultivate; the pace of daily life and the looming deadlines and social obligations consumed my moments of stillness.

I was sitting at my desk one evening with my face blankly resting over a spreadsheet, the stress increasing. I started to take shallow breaths, my shoulders tensed up, and the anxious rush was beginning. A memory surfaced, Rudra's voice, steady and calm and then I collapsed back into sleep. "Does the river fight when it meets a rock? No. It flows around it."

So, I took a deep breath, taking in the air, and let the air go out of my mouth, my lungs free of pressure Breathing was my connection to this infinite. Whether the surface was chaotic or not, it didn't matter, to the current was the same.

Upon opening my eyes, the tension was gone. Deadlines remained, the spreadsheet was still there, but they didn't seem insurmountable anymore. I could go round them, through them, with them. This rock was not an obstacle, it was part of the journey.

The Challenge of Integration

It was not easy living the wisdom of the mountains in the heart of the city. Stability, compassion, discernment, courage, introspection, creation, and surrender were not things to be idealized at a distance; they were something to put one's arms around and embody. They were like any practice, that is, requiring effort, patience, as well as persistence.

The hardest at first was stability. The city was fast-paced and easy to get swept up in the currents of external demands to the point where you might lose your footing. With each morning, I started off with a grounding ritual I adapted from Adira's stability—a few minutes of meditation focusing on breath, and the feeling of my feet against the floor. This was a little act but it reminded me that if I wanted to be stable then the stability was within me and not around me.

The next major challenge was: compassion. Surrounded by the calm presence of the monks in the mountains, I could so easily connect with others. It was even more challenging for me in the city, where tempers flared and patience wore thin. Kindness often felt like a transaction, and genuine connection was lost in the rush of daily life. Yet, I reminded myself—true compassion wasn't about external circumstances; it was about maintaining an open heart, even in the face of resistance.

Sharing the Flow

Weeks went by and I started to notice something different. The mountains weren't teaching me those lessons alone. They were filling my inner world, and rippling like water out into the world around me.

One evening a friend of mine called, crying, overwhelmed by too much work. She was, after all, having trouble keeping herself together, and her voice trembled as she finished.

I gave her the space to talk, without interrupting. When she finished, I shared a simple truth I had learned: "Now you will understand that you don't need to scratch the current, do you? Just breathe, just step. That is why the river always finds its way."

On the other end of the line, she said nothing, but she didn't need to. Finally, she said, "Thank you. I needed to hear that."

It wasn't a grand or a profound thing, but it felt right. The river's wisdom was spreading out, ripples of it.

That one evening, the city had already become part of its rhythm of night, I was sitting by my window, watching the lights stretching endlessly afar. Monks' stones sat on the windowsill, their semi-conspicuous presence a reminder of the journey I had taken.

There was a river within me now, the river calm and unmoving. I did not need to remember the monks' wisdom, it was becoming something I lived in every moment, in every breath.

The journey wasn't over. It never would be. Yet, for the first time, I realized that the road wasn't about getting anywhere. That was crossing over, being fully present, being fully alive, taking each step, one of the infinites.

I sat there, the noises of the city merging with the stillness of my soul but with a quiet kind of peace. Transformation ripples had started and the journey had just begun.

Inspiring the Flow

As the sun dipped into the horizon, painting the sky with hues of crimson and violet, I strolled along the Juhu beach in Mumbai, the salty air filling my lungs. The distant roar of the waves crashing against the bare rocks echoed through the air, reminiscent of Ganga's soothing voice. My elder son, Arhum, knelt by the water's edge, engrossed in building a sandcastle. With each wave, his creation would crumble, only for him to begin anew. His persistence and quiet determination drew me in.

As I watched, a lesson Rudra had once shared came to mind: "Resistance is not about defiance, but adaptation." The rocks in the river, worn smooth by the constant flow, were a testament to this wisdom.

Arhum looked up, his face a mix of frustration and sand. "It keeps getting broken by the waves," he said, his voice laced with despair. I knelt beside him, running my fingers through the sand.

"Maybe the waves aren't breaking it," I said gently. "Maybe they're shaping it differently." Arhum's skepticism was palpable, but together we began to rebuild the castle, this time farther back from the waterline. As the gentler waves lapped at the shore, the castle stood firm, its walls a testament to our collaboration. Wonder sparkled in Arhum's eyes, and a broad smile spread across his face.

"Thank you," he said softly, his voice filled with gratitude. As we walked away, I realized that this simple interaction had reflected the wisdom I'd been learning to incorporate into my life. It wasn't about grand gestures or dramatic displays; it was about being present, moving with the flow of life, and taking action with intention.

The Power of Sharing

I couldn't keep the wisdom of Adira, Ishani, Kapeesh, Sarthak, Varya, Vyom, Rudra, the river, and mountains to myself. This wasn't something to be hoarded as if it were a secret treasure, but to flow out to touch others and to inspire their own journey.

So, one Saturday morning I gathered a group of friends for what I called a "Flow Session" at a Park. The idea was simple: to get in touch with nature, consider the rhythms of life, and look for our own moments of silence in the noise of the city.

To start, we explored through the forest, a few of us walking so quietly that the sound of leaves crunching while we walked and the sound of birds chirping overhead seemed to almost be nothingness. I asked everyone to sit in silence and listen, not just to what the wind blows in, but to the internal flow. We sat by a small clearing by a stream.

"What do you hear?" I asked after a while.

One friend replied: "The stream. It's soothing."

"The wind," said another. "It's constant."

"And within you?" I pressed.

Their faces were thoughtful, they hesitated. Someone finally said my breath. "It's… steady."

I told them that's the flow. "First, they guide the stream and the wind with the same rhythm. It's always there. You just have to tune in."

That morning, we reflected, shared, and were together. At the end of the session, everyone became quiet and more centered—they hadn't been that way when they started. While parting ways one friend hugged me and she said, "I didn't realize how much I needed this."

"Neither had I.", I said in my mind. Sharing the wisdom to create space for others to connect with themselves and come back to themselves felt like an extension of my own journey. I was beginning to see that the river's flow was not one completed by me but through me unto others.

Moments of Doubt

Not every day was seamless. Sometimes, the weight of life was starting to pull me down. There were deadlines to meet, relationships to mend and the city's never-ending pace sometimes to me smothering. In the mountains, I had cultivated some stillness, and that felt so far away.

On a particularly tough evening, where this colleague and I had just had an even tougher discussion, I sat down on my floor, in my apartment, filled with rage and frustration. Doubt, anger, and urges to control every part of my life came back.

But then I remembered Rudra's words, the embodiment of surrender: It doesn't fight the rocks, it flows around them.

I focused on my breath and closed my eyes. Inhale. Exhale. Inhale. Exhale. The chaos within me started to settle, slowly. The tension was still there, and the argument was still unresolved, but something new was crackling. I didn't have to struggle with this situation. I simply trusted the current would take me somewhere, and that I could flow alongside it.

The next day, I went to my colleague, with an open heart and openness to hear. Instead, what might have become an extended conflict became an opportunity for understanding and growth. Yet, the rock was still there and I now knew how to flow around it.

The Infinite Flow

Months passed, and I became more aware of this flow, from a small event of how the traffic lights changed from green to red, to how I could connect with loved ones during every pause. It wasn't confined to the river, or the mountains, it was woven into the fabric of being.

One night I started to meditate by candlelight and felt a great deal of gratitude. They weren't just memories of the journey I had taken to the mountains, after learning from the monks, the wisdom of Adira's stability, Ishani's compassion, Kapeesh's discernment, Sarthak's courage, Varya's introspection, Vyom's creativity, and Rudra's surrender. They were alive in me and I lived and moved through the world their way.

I mused on the monks, their silent presence, and these profound teachings. I pictured the current of the river unyielding, and infinite. I thought of how hundreds of lives flowed from that, each a ripple in the endless sea of existence and I remembered.

It wasn't a journey of going someplace, but walking it, step by step, with an open heart and willingness to flow. As I sat there, the flickering candlelight dancing on the walls, I felt a quiet certainty: I knew the river inside me had been flowing; it always would.

A Closing Prayer

Finally closing the final words of this book, I have much gratitude for the ride and the lessons and to you, the reader, who traveled this road with me through these pages. Just to end this story I'll offer a prayer that has been a guiding light, a source of peace and solace along the journey, not goodbye, but connection.

This Shanti mantra is said in the ancient tongue of Sanskrit and speaks of universal well-being, harmony, and the ceasing of suffering. It's a wish for all the beings, also for you, but also a blessing.

सर्वे भवन्तु सुखिनः सर्वे सन्तु निरामयाः। सर्वे भद्राणि पश्यन्तु मा कश्चिद् दुःखभाग्भवेत्। ॐ शान्तिः शान्तिः शान्तिः॥

May all beings be happy. May everyone be free of illness. May all be auspicious unto them to see. May no one suffer. May the peace be with you.

With this prayer, I thank you from the bottom of my heart for taking a hike with me. All that the river has been and the mountains have been silently and the bits of light that we've extracted together — they now belong to you as much as they belong to me.

I wish you lots of flow in life. May you accept the tides of challenges and joy with grace. And we wish that your path never strays from you to the knowledge of the infinite within yourself.

Thank you for participating in this journey – for being here, for trusting and allowing this to unfold.

Om Shanti, Shanti, Shanti.

May the peace be with you.

ACKNOWLEDGMENTS

I sit here writing and reflecting on the journey that has put this book in my hands and I am overwhelmed with the number of people, moments, and blessings it took to make it possible. This acknowledgment is like trying to catch the wind in my hands; it's impossible to hold it all, but I want to try my best to honor those that have been part of this life path.

Rather, this is a mosaic of countless influences, moments of grace, and people who stayed by me (when I didn't even know I needed them) in order to make this one book. If you're reading this, then you play a part in this piece of this journey and for that, I am forever grateful.

To My Beloved Wife

For all, my deepest gratitude goes to my wife, Sabah.

You are the anchor in my storm, the calm in my chaos, and the constant light that never stops leading me home. Through the times when life felt like it was crumbling, when I doubted myself, when I couldn't see the road ahead you were there, standing beside me, with a quiet strength that no words on this earth can ever do justice to.

I think back to the moments just before I left for the Himalayas, the uncertainty, the fear, the pull of all that was unknown. It was ours, or at least that's what I remember it being. And yet, you didn't stop me, because you knew I had to find something — then or some other time — even if nobody had any clue exactly what that was.

You have been my greatest blessings in patience, faith, and love. Thank you for holding space for me; believing in me even when I couldn't; and being my greatest teacher in love, resilience, and most importantly grace.

To My Two Little Sons

To my two wonderful boys Arhum and Aarish, as much as I write this book for anyone else, I am writing it for you too.

You'll still be too young to fully understand all of this now, but I hope one day you'll read these pages and find more than the story of your father, more of the lessons I learned along the way, and maybe even some that'll guide you on your own journeys.

And Arhum, your curiosity, your boundless energy makes me want to see the world afresh, to ask questions and to keep asking questions, and to keep exploring. Rest in power to Aarish, your quiet wisdom, and compassion remind me of the power of stillness, listening, and being present.

Both of you have taught me so much about life that I don't have words enough to write. Thanks for being my mirror, my joy, and my biggest reason for growing.

Acknowledgments

To My Mother: The Source of Endless Love

To my dearest mother, god, you are the foundation of all that I am and all that I wish to be. You were my first teacher, you were with me from the very beginning, you taught me without lectures or lessons, just a pure form of love, patience, and selflessness. You've been the light guiding me as I endure life's most brutal moments of trial and tribulations. What you taught me is, that resilience isn't about never breaking, it's about rising every time stronger and wiser. Your warmth and tenderness kept our home where love and understanding have always been the case.

In all my life I nevertheless thought about all of the sacrifices you had made for me; of those things I only came to understand the hard way when I became older. You bled yourself out for me to have the means to go out and get to know this planet, even if it cost your own dreams. One of the greatest sources of my inspiration was your unassuming beauty under pressure. Every lesson I've learned in these pages finds its root in the values you instilled in me: compassion, humility, and an absolute and unshakeable belief that people are good. I thank you for being my anchor, my compass always to guide me towards the light.

To My Father: Strength and Wisdom Legacy

To the memory of my late father to whom I can never give back enough, but whose absence I feel always, and whose presence still leads me in ways I cannot put into words. You were not just a parent; you were the mentor; you were the role model; you were the one to lift me higher. You taught me your wisdom, your teaching of the world, of the value of integrity as the most valued of all currencies in a person. You were a living example of strength and you taught me your strength comes not from a dominant position but from humility and a heart to serve others.

I have your lessons that I carry with me, lessons which I now know were the bare foundations of my journey. You encouraged, praised, believed in and most importantly, loved me. Though you are no longer here in a physical sense, I feel you are here every time I decide to take a step. You will always be remembered in your memory and the legacy of values you left behind; this book, this journey, is dedicated to you. I thank you, Dad, for teaching me to dream big, but also to be seated with feet planted firmly in the ground.

To My Friends: My Chosen Family

You are the unsung heroes of my life. Each of you are my pillars of support, a wellspring of wisdom, and a source of laughter when I needed it the most. Whenever I felt like I lost my worth, you reminded me. In your times of triumph, I celebrated yours as I would have my own. It's you who are my chosen family, you who see me as I am, and as much as I can be.

I can't thank you enough for walking with me through the highs and the lows, the certainties and the chaos. Whether it was through conversations at midnight, adventures together, or moments of understanding, your name symbolized the beauty of a human connection. I may have written this book under my name, but it's full of the echoes of our shared memories, lessons, and experiences. I thank you all, each of you, for being my safe harbor and my co-traveler on this extraordinary journey of life.

Acknowledgments

To My Mentor and Guru

I am perpetually indebted to my mentor and guru for his support on this journey and who has been a distant guiding star throughout my life.

Your teachings have been the bedrock upon which I have traveled — the compass to true nor a path of self-discovery. You have shown me through your wisdom that we must take the most incredible journeys within ourselves.

But you've always told me, 'The path will be yours to walk, but it doesn't mean you will be alone.' Those words have been a lifeline, a silent reminder that I wasn't alone: that that something existed beyond my own flesh and bones implying me.

Thank you for your patience, thank you for all the guidance, and thank you for believing in me, even when I couldn't see it myself.

To the Seven Monks

How do you thank people whose work so fundamentally changes the core of who you are? You weren't just seven monks; you were a universal truth I had ignored because I had been too busy to notice. Your stillness was a lesson it taught itself louder than any words could ever be. As you were present, I saw my being dissolved, the false constructions of my ego, and the still quietness of my soul.

Because you knew I had the answers already you didn't give me any. You didn't teach me what to do, instead, you held space for me to face my fears, challenge my beliefs and extricate me from my own mind's clutter, to reveal the truths buried within. I was blessed with a fragment of wisdom from each of you, not necessarily an obligation, but a gift freely given that set the foundation for my being.

Thank you for having patience for me as I stumbled, compassion for me as I resisted and for your presence as I slowly understood. And you are wrong, your silence was not an empty space, it was a sacred mirror that reflected the stillness I needed to see within myself. You taught me that the path to take wasn't to search somewhere else; it was to retrieve that which existed within all along.

To Rudra

It (Smiling Through the Pain) was also my Mirror, my Guide, my Catalyst.

Rudra, where do I even begin? You were not only a guide, you were a force, alchemy of wisdom, provocation, truth, and you shook me to my core. When I first met you there was something — there was something relentless, something that wouldn't let me hide from myself.

You pushed me to the edges of my comfort and made me look myself in the face not only of the hurdles that guard the path ahead but the ones I cut for myself. I can't forget what you did, shoving me into the icy waters of the Ganga by the river. How could I not have noticed? How could this be happening? Why is this happening? I found clarity through the chaos, through that moment of surrender. I found myself.

You showed me that life isn't about shielding yourself from the cold, it's about jumping into it head first, feeling it, adapting to it. Your lessons were not soft, they were raw, unapologetic, and altogether transformative. You challenged me, everything I thought I was and with that, allowed me to find the infinite in me.

I thank you for your humor that made me forget my hatred, your silence that made me think of my death, and your wisdom that let me guide myself. You didn't just show me the way; you became the way. You also reminded me the entire time that the destination wasn't the goal. It's always been, always is, and always will be the purpose is the journey.

To the Mountains and the Ganga: My Silent Teachers

But how does one take something so vast, so eternal, so alive and say thank you? The Himalayas were not mere mountains they were sentinels of truth, guardians of a silence that erased me and reconstructed me. Whether you knew it or not, you were my refuge and my reckoning, forcing me to face my ego's smallness against the size of everything.

Your peaks told of the strength of surviving and the strength to survive and of the humbleness of standing still amidst something infinitely bigger than one's own self. You expected nothing of me, though you gave me perspective, clarity, and a sense of belonging to something much greater than myself.

And then there was the Ganga. You can't just say my waters carried me, my waters healed me, my waters shaped me, my waters returned me to myself. You relentless, unrelenting, yet tender, held my doubts and fears, and washed them away. You reminded me that surrender is not in weakness, it's in strength, flow is not a luxury, it's a must, and life's rhythm comes from trust, not resistance.

Dear Ganga, you were not just a river but a teacher, a guide reminding us how infinite the lake can be if you allow yourself to flow. Thank you for holding me, teaching me, and showing me that the path isn't about the current, it's about becoming the flow.

To You, the Reader

Thank you from the bottom of my heart. I very much appreciate you for being on this path and coming into these pages with curiosity, open heart, and courage. This book is more than a sharing of my journey, it's a call to yours. Each of these words, each of these lessons, every moment I've shared here was written with the barest hope that it would speak to a part of your soul, the part that wants to ache for something more, for something infinite.

You didn't just read my story; you held space for it. You let it encounter your own experiences, your own questions, your own truths and you let it all in. It's yours just as much as it's mine because a story only breathes once it is told, once it is shared once it is felt, felt through the eyes of someone else's story.

I wish above all that these pages reminded you of your quiet stillness, that this courage inside you has quietly, persistently been

Acknowledgments

burning, and that what is possible is infinite when you dare to listen to whispers of your soul.

That willingness to journey into the unknown, to face the shadows, to go into the light is just a testament to the strength and beauty of the human spirit. I am grateful you had faith that I would walk alongside you, even if only for a little while. It's a never-ending journey within, but it gets more prosperous, deeper, and more meaningful bit by bit.

When you're closing this book or when you're sick of whatever we're doing now, know that you're never really alone. If you follow the flow of life, you are always guided by the infinite, the wisdom you have within. Thank you for being on this journey with me. May the light, love, and the strength to flow endlessly forward find your path.

APPENDIX

Activations for walking the inner journey.

Before you close this book, I want to end with something you can use on your journey forward, a set of tools that served me to navigate my own path and serves as a kind of anchor for me every day. Inspired by the stillness of the mountains, (and) the flow of the river, (we learn using) these practices. They are simple and profound and intended as a way to bring these lessons into your own life.

Consider these tools to be invitations, not rules — invitations to connect with your inner stillness and the flow of life, invitations to live with meaning in the act of living ordinary moments that are the miracle of the journey of life. These tools as gentle guides—reminders to pause, breathe, and reconnect with the deeper rhythm of life. They are stepping stones, not destinations, leading you back to the wisdom that already resides within you.

When to Use It:

1. In moments of stress, overwhelm, or uncertainty.
2. To center yourself before a big decision or conversation.
3. As a daily practice to bring balance and clarity into your life.

Exercise / Process

1. The Breath: Your Anchor in the Storm

The breath is how we are taught by the monks as our most powerful tool: a bridge between the mind and body that is ever-present. The key to its rhythm is calm, clarity, and connection.

How to Practice Conscious Breathing:

1. Find a Quiet Space: Sit back, make yourself comfortable, or lie on your back if it feels better.
2. Inhale Deeply: Inhale through your nose for a count of four, feel your stomach expand.
3. Hold for Stillness: Count to four and feel the stillness really come into your being.
4. Exhale Slowly: If you time it right, you can think of the five seconds as breathing first out your mouth for a count of six, releasing all the tension you have at that moment.
5. Repeat: Practice for five to ten minutes or as long as you need it to feel grounded.·

2. Gratitude: Shifting Your Perspective

Gratitude is both more than and less than an emotion—it is a new way to view the world. If you're grateful, you will see not only more reasons to be grateful but you will view the world very differently.

How to Practice Gratitude Journaling:

1. Choose Your Medium: In other words, just use something: a notebook, a digital journal, or even just scrap paper.

2. Set a Time: Also do 5–10 minutes each day writing about what you're grateful for. Morning or evening is great.
3. Write Three Things: You note three specific things that you are grateful for that day. A kind word might be the smallest, but it can also be the breakthrough.
4. Feel It: Write and feel the gratitude.

   Why It Matters:

   Gratitude pulls your attention away from the things that are missing and toward all that is available. It helps you to be able to see lessons in the challenges and beauty in the mundane.

3. The Art of Presence: Mindful Observation

The stillness and power of these mountains taught me something else about the power of observation – how to see the world without being judgmental; how to just be.

How to Practice Mindful Observation:

1. Select an Object: It could be a leaf, a candle, or your morning coffee.
2. Engage Fully: See it close, as you haven't seen it before. Give it notice of its colors, its textures, and the way that it moves.
3. Use All Your Senses: What does it feel like, smell like, what does it sound like?
4. Stay Present: Simply bring to bear your mind on the object — whenever it strays, unwind and gently reconfigure it on the object.· Especially when you're distracted or disconnected.· For the times that you get stressed.· It's a way to appreciate life in a small way.

4. Transforming the Mundane: Repetitive Task Practice

Moving rocks and fetching water were repetitive tasks for the monks, which taught me the beauty of presence and brought me some of the most important lessons on the simplest of acts.

How to Create Your Own Practice:

1. Choose a Task: Choose something easy, such as folding clothes, sweeping the floor, or washing dishes.
2. Be Fully Present: Concentrate on each movement and each sensation.
3. Let Go of Judgment: Just don't rush into the task and don't call it trivial.
4. Reflect: Ask yourself: 'What is this task teaching me about patience, presence, or acceptance?'

Why It's Transformative:

When looked at it with mindfulness, there is not an ordinary moment in your life. It recasts the banal into meditation.

5. Embracing Dualities: Finding Balance

On the dance of life between opposites; inside and outside, stillness and movement, light and shadow. The answer is really both.

How to Cultivate Balance:

1. Acknowledge Your Dualities: Ask yourself to think about areas of tension in your life, work vs. rest, giving vs. receiving, and so forth.

2. Create Space for Both: Honor both sides of the duality and dedicate time to that.
3. Use Breath as a Bridge: When things are off. Find your breath and get back in balance.
4. Practice Acceptance: Recognize opposites instead of resisting their pull, and recognize that they are necessary parts of a whole.

6. Nature as a Teacher: Reconnecting with the Earth

Nature reminded me that we are not separate from nature: you must be me because I am you.

1. How to Reconnect with Nature: Spend Time Outdoors: Whatever your setup—be it a park or forest or balcony—connect with the natural world.
2. Observe and Listen: Feel the rhythms of nature, the sound of water, the rustling of leaves, and the chirping of the birds.
3. Seek Lessons: Consider what nature is teaching you about patience, or about impermanence, or about growth.
4. Express Gratitude: Recognize the earth as your ally, as your teacher, as the source of nourishment.

7. Rituals: Creating Meaningful Moments

The monks lived simply while living intentionally, having rituals in their day that had meaning. You can make your own customized one for you and your individualized life.

How to Create Your Rituals:

1. Start Small: Pick one practice for the day: either morning meditation or with an evening journal.

2. Infuse Intention: Have focus and purpose to approach the ritual, make it a sacred act.
3. Be Consistent: Practice daily in order to create rhythm and grounding.
4. Adapt as You Grow: Allow your rituals to breathe with you, to gradually transform in line with yours.

A Final Thought

These are not tools that will lead you to perfection, or crossing things off a list. Day after day, they are about showing up for yourself with curiosity and compassion. What they are about is walking the path not to an end but with the goal of deepening your connection with the path itself.

Keep these practices with you as ones to come along. In moments of doubt, let them hold you, anchor you in times of chaos, and remind you of all the infinite wisdom you already possess within.

Bonus Gift for Readers

Your Exclusive Invitation: A Special Gift for You

Your journey through The Silent Path: A Journey Within is just the beginning. True transformation isn't just about understanding—it's about applying these insights into your daily life, experiencing inner stillness even amidst the noise.

To support you in deepening your journey, I want to personally invite you to a FREE 90-minute session, where we will explore:

- How to integrate stillness into everyday life
- Practical techniques for mental clarity and emotional resilience
- The deeper lessons from my journey that I couldn't fit into the book

How to Access Your Free Masterclass

1. Visit https://thesilentpath.mindarchitect.in
2. Enter the exclusive reader code: IAPPROVEOFMYSELF
3. Gain instant access to the training + additional surprise bonuses

This is my way of thanking you for embarking on this journey with me. I hope this masterclass helps you apply these teachings in a way that transforms your life, just as they did mine.

I look forward to seeing you inside. Let's walk this path together.

With gratitude,

Cherag Shah

www.ingramcontent.com/pod-product-compliance
Lightning Source LLC
LaVergne TN
LVHW041915070526
838199LV00051BA/2621